Preaching

Preaching

Preparation and Performance

by

Brian H. Butler

Marshall Pickering

Marshall Morgan and Scott
Marshall Pickering
34 42 Cleveland Street, London W1P 5FB

First published in 1989 by Marshall Morgan and Scott Publications Ltd.
Part of the Marshall Pickering Holdings Group

ISBN: 0 551 01792-9

Text Set in Baskerville by Prima Graphics, Camberley, Surrey
Printed in Great Britain by Anchor Press, Colchester, Essex

Contents

To my students,
past and present

Preface

There have been two approaches to the study of preaching (or homiletics, to give it the technical name). One says that preaching is basically a gift, and there is little that one can do to impart skill in preaching. This was the view of Dr D. M. Lloyd-Jones, an undoubted giant of pulpit power, who stated in a lecture on 'Preachers and Preaching':

> What about preaching as such, the act of preaching of which I have spoken? There is only one thing to say about this; it cannot be taught. That is impossible. Preachers are born, not made. This is an absolute. You will never teach a man to be a preacher if he is not already one.

Pretty strong stuff; and hardly something to encourage anyone who presumes to write about homiletics. (He calls books on homiletics 'an abomination'.)

Now no one can deny the force of the argument, although it seems to favour the giants (of whom, of course, the doctor was one), but does little to encourage mere mortals, who are much more numerous. I assume that the vast majority of those who look at this book will be ones who feel their inadequacy, and would like to feel it less by learning as much as possible about the business of making sermons.

The other approach to preaching, whilst not denying that it rests upon a gift, maintains that it is possible to develop that gift by learning a craft. It was a belief held by Charles Simeon (1759–1836), the great Anglican preacher whose Cambridge ministry extended over some forty years. 'Simeon was almost the first man in the history of the English pulpit since the

Middle Ages to appreciate that it is perfectly possible to teach men how to preach, and to discover how to do so,' is the considered judgment of Charles Smyth, the author of the standard book on preaching in the Church of England (see Bibliography). Simeon's method of teaching was to gather Cambridge students in his house on Friday evenings for informal sessions at which they produced sermon outlines and discussed them together.

Since I use the illustration of the concert pianist a great deal in this book, let me bring him in here. I do not doubt for a moment that a great pianist is born and not made. He needs a heaven-sent *gift* to provide that extra something which will mark him out from the crowd of aspiring pianists. But the concert pianist was never yet born who did not practise for hours and hours and hours. When you read about the vigorous regime of study of the budding pianist, it makes you feel exhausted. My thought in pondering the immense labour that the concert pianist puts into his preparation and performance is often: Why do so many of us preachers work at our task so little, or so perfunctorily? We have a nobler work, a more abundant reward, and an ultimately more satisfying life. Yet we tire, and become discouraged so easily. My hope is that this book will motivate preachers to work at their preaching, and to work hard.

I am aware that there are many people preaching today who have no formal training. They have not had the opportunity of a full-time course at a theological college, but they do have the opportunity to preach. I have written with them very much in mind, whilst also hoping to help the average Bible College student. I personally have always profited by reading books on peaching, and I hope that this book will appeal to those who have been preaching for some years, but who might benefit from a reflection once again upon basic principles.

And I am also aware that among the company of preachers nowadays are many women. Some churches have always welcomed women preachers – 'My best men are women', said General Booth, and John Wesley *could* have said something similar. Other Churches have been much slower to recognise that some women have a gift for preaching, but are now beginning to change their minds. I don't wish to enter into the argument. But if there are to be women preachers then they too need instruction of the kind I aim to provide. But the gender question does present an author with a problem. It is not helpful if a writer has to keep saying, 'He (or she)...' and it is very clumsy to say, 'One should...' all the time. So I have used the masculine gender throughout simply because the vast majority of preachers are still male, and without any slight to whatever feminine readers I have (and I hope they are many!). I might add that during many years of teaching homiletics to students, and hearing them preach, the women have outshone the men on numerous occasions.

One further disclaimer needs mentioning. I am aware that sometimes my advice will seem very 'black and white'. It will certainly seem so to any experienced preacher who happens to read the book. Once again, I can only say that I wanted to avoid constant qualification, which can become very irritating and, to the learner, somewhat confusing. Better, it seems to me, to say what I think is best, and then leave the reader to prove or disprove it in his own experience – which he will. As Alec Motyer has said to me, 'Every man should find his own brand of murder – and practise it!'

Like most Christian topics, that of preaching arouses strong feelings, and widely differing viewpoints. My main concern is that those starting out on the road of preaching should learn the basics according to what may be termed classical principles. Once that has been done, then any amount of experimentation is in order. Just as a doctor learns anatomy, physiology and pathology before he ever operates on an actual human body, so I believe that a preacher needs to learn the rudiments of homiletics thoroughly before he abandons them and strikes out along unaccustomed paths. My convictions about this are founded on the observation of several hundred students and a multitude of other preachers. The rambling, unstructured and thoroughly dull sermons that are frequently inflicted on long-suffering congregations suggest that many preachers have not learned the basics properly, and sadly, many seem to despise them.

Perhaps I ought to comment on my title, *Preaching:*

Preparation and Performance. Some people may well hold up their hands in horror. Preaching a performance! The very idea! I can only plead that my purpose in using it was to allow me to make the comparison between the concert pianist and the preacher, which underlies much of what I have to say about the preaching task. I am aware that preaching is a world removed from a concert performance. Yet insofar as it is done in public with the aim of absorbing listeners in the great music of the Gospel, the analogy is, I believe, valuable enough to keep.

It only remains to thank the preachers who have inspired me in my own preaching, the writers with whom I have conducted a continuing conversation, and my students in Nigeria and England whom it has been my privilege to teach. And I am particularly grateful to the Rev. Alec Motyer, my own parish minister, who read the manuscript, offered excellent advice from his stores of wisdom, and, not least, provides his congregation with such a consistently high level of preaching week by week, and thus exemplifies many of the ideals I have tried to expound in these pages.

'A minister of the Word who writes about preaching writes as a learner to other learners and like them he is haunted by the sermon that no one is great enough to preach' (R. E. C. Browne). That expresses perfectly the spirit in which these pages are sent out.

Introduction

I've played the piano for many years. Amidst the daily concerns and pressures of the ministry, I've found that sitting down at the keyboard has brought release. Music has a power to absorb the mind and heart completely, taking us into a world which not only is different from the everyday one where we normally live, but which often substitutes cosmos for chaos. Music is the most spiritual and non-material of all the arts, and to the music-lover it is not surprising that so much is said about it in Scripture, as a source of comfort as well as a means of worship on earth and in heaven.

I have also enjoyed listening to the great pianists of past and present on radio and record. The piano repertoire is so vast and rich that there are always new tracts to be explored, or old places to be re-visited.

Over the years I have read quite a lot of what pianists have had to say about their work. The more I read, the more it becomes apparent that what they say about playing the piano reflects much the same concerns I have in preaching. The preacher and the professional concert pianist have almost identical aims. For them both their work has two aspects – *preparation* in private behind closed doors, and public *performance*.

In the beginning was the Word. Every preacher must start there, looking afresh at the Word of God written, hoping that it will become a living word for him and his hearers. Every preacher worth his salt is a life-long student of the Holy Bible. Martyn Lloyd-Jones, that giant among 20th-century preachers, said that a preacher should at the very least read the Bible through each year in its entirety.

For the pianist, there is a similar sanctity about the score. It also stands before him with absolute authority, compelling heart and mind to seek out its truth and to obey its message.

Then for both preacher and the musician, there is the labour of fashioning a message from the text. The preacher speaks about sermon preparation, the pianist about practising. Both are after the same thing – complete mastery of the text with which they have begun, so that it yields up its secret. 'In labours oft,' says Paul. As I've read of the hours, days and years that go into the making of a pianist's repertoire, I have frequently been ashamed at the time I've been prepared to spend to become a better preacher.

Then for both preacher and pianist there is a public performance. Some preachers might not like the idea of preaching being called a performance. Perhaps it isn't. There is a divine authority inherent in preaching, a 'Thus says the Lord' quality in the best preaching which is compelling in a way that no musical performance can be. Nevertheless, I believe the parallel may be made. One thing is certain. It is doubtful whether any preacher climbs the pulpit stairs having laboured over his sermons, or crafted them with such persistence, as the concert pianist has his programme.

These, then, are the two aspects of preaching and pianism which I have found it helpful to ponder: private preparation and public performance.

I think it would be helpful for the beginner preacher to have the material for homiletics divided in this way. I have divided the material into two halves – practice and performance – so that the reader can turn to whatever section he needs. Throughout I have aimed at simplicity. I have in mind those who want to preach but have very little idea how to go about it. Discussion of homiletic theory has, therefore, been kept to a minimum, although every preacher should have at least some understanding of what he is trying to accomplish before he ever starts to preach.

Nor do I want to exclude experienced preachers from listening in to what I have to say. As a preacher, I've always opened a book on preaching with a sense of expectation, conscious that I have never been able to claim to have arrived at excellence in the art and craft, but only of being a learner. I'm always looking for new secrets, new methods which will give me better tools for the job. Whether a book is for apprentices or craftsmen, it is rarely that I have been disappointed in finding something that challenged, rebuked or instructed. I can only hope that the same is true for those who pick up this book with the same hope.

Part I

Preparation

Thinking about it

As a pilgrim travels from the City of Destruction to the Celestial City, every so often he receives exhortation from a fellow-traveller. He needs encouragement, warming and food for the journey ahead. Most pilgrims stop once or twice a week for such refreshment and reflection, and the innkeeper who supplies their need is the preacher. (Let us assume every preacher is a Christian.)

But the innkeeper also needs to ask himself from time to time, 'What about this menu I'm setting before these pilgrims week after week? Is it meeting their needs? Is it being prepared properly?'

What is preaching?

The question 'what is preaching?' has been endlessly discussed, as frequently and possibly as fruitlessly as the question, 'What is sociology?' or 'What is Art?' In fact, like the question 'Is there a God?', no answer is given in Scripture, which suggests that the question may be as pointless in the one case as the other. When we ask 'What is preaching?' we are not seeking a theoretical answer so much as trying to answer the question 'What is preaching supposed to be doing?'

We can hardly quarrel with Campbell Morgan's statement that 'The supreme work of the Christian minister is the work of preaching' (Morgan, p. 11). It is a reminder that whatever other tasks fall to the lot of the minister – whether administration, visitation, counselling, or whatever else – nothing should displace preaching as the minister's supreme concern. And in these days when others in the Church are being given the opportunity to preach, and plurality of elders is becoming commonplace, we need to ensure that whoever is called upon to preach has a proper sense of the high dignity and importance of preaching in the life of the Church.

Firstly, preaching has the high place in Christianity that it does (in contrast to other religions, incidentally) because preaching is a proclamation of the Word of God. Just as at the heart of our faith lies the conviction about the Word made flesh, so at the centre of preaching is the endeavour to unfold the Word of God in scripture in human words. In preaching, there is a divine-human encounter that reflects God's reaching out to the human race in revelation and redemption.

Secondly, preaching has always had an important place in God's dealings with men. The Old Testament had its prophets, the New Testament had its apostles and missionaries, and supremely 'Jesus came preaching' (Mark 1:14). Its great importance through the biblical period has been reflected in subsequent history. Even a cursory reading of Church history reveals that periods of vitality and advance have invariably been accompanied by increased activity in the field of preaching – the 13th-century Renewal associated with Francis and Dominic, the Reformation, and the Evangelical Revival in England under the Wesleys and George Whitefield come immediately to mind.

Thirdly, preaching has never been displaced as the most important means of Christian instruction and especially as the means of conversion. This might be disputed on two fronts. Some would want to place the Eucharist, or Lord's Supper, in the central place as the supreme activity of the Church, and as the chief means of grace. Without detracting from its import- ance in any way, or denying its centrality in the Church's worship, it is nevertheless true that the Lord's Supper only has its rightful place when set side by side with an emphasis (equal or greater is debatable) on biblical preaching. It was John Wesley, one of the greatest preachers in the history of the Church, who spoke of the Holy Communion as a 'converting ordinance' but who nevertheless transformed religion in England by his preaching. It is possible to set preaching and the Sacraments in opposition, where they are more rightly seen as complementary.

Recent years have seen an immense growth of home Bible

study groups and small growth groups in all denominations. They have proved so fruitful, and have transformed the lives of so many, that it could be argued that they are more influential at the present time than the pulpit. Preaching undoubtedly occupies a lesser place in Christendom than it did one or two generations ago. Without entering into a full discussion of all the issues involved, one might assume that most Christians feel a need for the kind of participation and fellowship that small groups provide. They are no longer satisfied with being passive hearers – they want to get involved with their own spiritual development and to enjoy the personal sharing of Bible study which they find in home groups. This is all to the good, and it is no good trying to be a Canute to the present flow of the tide. But it is important to note that in churches where small growth groups have been most successful, strong preaching tends to be the rule rather than the exception. Again, as with the Eucharist, there need be no contradiction between the two. In both cases, the need is for better preaching, not less preaching.

When we are tempted to lower the profile of preaching, we should remind ourselves of its place in the Bible, in history and in our own experience. A moment's reflection will convince us that it is impossible to exaggerate its importance. And the result should be to make us determined to become better preachers. The reason why people in the pew become impatient with preaching is usually because the preacher himself gives the impression that it is unimportant to him too. He may have grown tired of the labour it demanded to do it well, or have been deflected from his priorities by current modes of thinking. He may have become discouraged at the meagre results that his preaching seems to produce, or failed to feed his own soul. The causes of devaluation are many and various. Often the remedy is to go and hear a really great preacher – preferably in person, or if that is not possible, then by means of a cassette. Preachers need to hear preachers, if only because fire strikes fire. Or take down a volume of sermons and read something by one of the past masters of the pulpit. This will quicken our resolution to preach again. Personally, I have never read a book on preaching which didn't inspire me to say, 'I ought to be doing a better job.' As George Sweazey says,

'Preachers learn to preach by studying those who do it well.'

Definitions of preaching are endless. This one, by Daniel Baumann, has always seemed to me to be as good a working definition as any:

> Preaching is the communication of biblical truth by man to men with the explicit purpose of eliciting behavioral change.

The latter part of Baumann's definition brings us to the very heart of our next question.

What am I trying to accomplish?

It has often struck me that many preachers fail in their preaching because they have never thought this question through sufficiently seriously. Perhaps in the busyness of their life they haven't taken time to sit down and reflect upon what they are doing. But this is rather like the painter who sits down in front of his canvas and has no idea what to paint.

W.P. Merrill says, 'We need to bear in mind that in preaching the object is even more important than the subject. Every sermon aims at definite action. It is meant to make a difference in the lives of the hearers, or it is no true sermon.'

When we reflect upon it, we may preach hundreds of sermons, each one based on a different topic or passage of scripture. Yet all of them have one basic aim – behavioural change. In that sense, what Merrill says is true: the object is more important than a multitude of subjects. So what am I trying to accomplish?

Listening

The Sovereign Lord has given me an instructed tongue,
  to know the word that sustains the weary.
He awakens me morning by morning,
  wakens my ear to listen like one being taught.

                                             Isaish 50:4

Isaiah's picture of the Servant of the Lord is a magnificent portrayal of the preacher. Before he becomes a speaker, he must a listener. Most of us are better at the first than the second. Simply because of the demands upon us to speak, we become facile speakers. We can come up with words at the drop of a hat. I remember a colleague warning me about the preacher's 'facile forties' when preaching is in danger of becoming second nature, and when he has done enough of it to lull him into the easy feeling that he knows how to do it reasonably well.

The only security against that attitude (surely a mortal disease) is to be a listener. To come to the Word of God, morning by morning, as a listener and as a learner. Not coming to the Word, as we have to do frequently, in search of texts for sermons, but as a listener to what the Lord has to say to us. We need to be taught no less than our congregations. And since we may sit under preaching irregularly ourselves, we need to sit under the preaching of the Word of God in the privacy of our devotional life particularly carefully.

The actual work of sermon preparation, however, also demands the same process of listening. Another snare of the preacher is to work out his themes and schemes without listening to the voice of the Spirit of God. This no doubt is the temptation of the more experienced preacher, rather than of the beginner. The danger is that we become dependent upon our experiences and skill as expositors, rather than being dependent upon the voice of God. We need to 'listen like one being taught' rather than like one who is teaching.

In the clamour of next Sunday's demands for a sermon, we are in danger of reaching for the pencil first and leaving the listening until later. But how necessary it is to allow the Word of God sufficient time to cut through our preoccupation with what we think are the church's needs, to listen to what the Spirit is saying to the churches. In the preacher's schedule there is no substitute for meditation – with all that this implies of slow, unhurried, prayerful thought in the presence of God about the passage before us. We can hardly complain that people won't listen to us, if we won't listen to God.

What is happening?

In these days of hot news and instant TV coverage, it is not difficult for the preacher to be aware of what is happening in the world. Indeed, for him as for others, the danger is not so much of being unaware, but of being so overwhelmed that he filters out the demands of the world 'out there'. Sometimes the news from around the world is so awful that we have to turn it off, being unable to bear the searing of our souls with the pain of the world.

However, the preacher who does not hear the sob of the creation, whether far or near, will be unable to minister the fullness of the Gospel of God's redeeming love. 'The chief end of preaching is comfort,' said Ian MacLean, a thought found also in R.W. Dale and James Denney.

As the preacher wrestles with the question 'What is happening?' he is imitating the age-old practice of the prophets of every age.

> I will stand at my watch
>   and station myself on the ramparts;
> I will look to see what he will say to me,
>   and what answer I am to give to this complaint.

Habakkuk 2:1

> One is calling to me from Seir,
>   'Watchman, what of the night?
>   Watchman, what of the night?'
>
> The watchman says:
>   'Morning comes, and also the night,
>   If you will inquire, inquire;
>   come back again.'

Isaiah 21:11–12 (RSV)

But if the preacher is to have his hand on the pulse of the world, he needs equally to have his ear open to the voice of God, to God's dealings with this doomed planet. It is the preacher's task to keep alive the awareness that amidst the wreckage of life, and the shattering of human hopes, God is active, and powerful still.

'Last night an angel of the God whose I am and whom I serve stood beside me and said, "Do not be afraid" . . . so keep up your courage, men.'

Acts 27:23-25

Men and women, tossed by the storms of life, still wait upon us for a word from the Lord of heaven that will instil new courage and banish fears. Only the man who has come from the presence of God with a fresh message has any authority to speak peace to the people.

What ought to be happening?

As well as the question 'What is happening?', the preacher will be asking the question 'What ought to be happening?' Even if he is not the pastor, the preacher will have some conception of where his church is going, or where it has come from, and where the areas of strength and weakness are. As he ponders his messages, there must be an underlying probing of areas of need in the church. Every preacher faces hearers who are as diverse as any group of people – old, young, middle-aged, rich and poor, clever or dull, educated and uneducated and with the vices and virtues common to most men. There will be a considerable range of spiritual experience and development. How can any sermon possibly deal with the needs of each and every one? Strange to say, the divine alchemy of the Holy Spirit, applying the timeless truths of Scripture, makes the impossible possible.

Knowing this, the preacher ought from time to time to ask some broader questions. He will not trust to chance in seeking to meet the needs of his congregation. He may well wish to explore the following questions:

Are there realms of Christian experience which are especially needful for our church at this time?

Have I neglected any areas of Christian doctrine? The words of James Reid are relevant here. He writes:

However elaborate our creed, the things we live by are very few. What are the central truths of the Gospel – the nature of Man, the greatness of God, the Fact of Sin, the Cross of

Calvary and the Redemption it purchased, the Power of the
Spirit, the Glory of the Church, and the Hope of His
Coming, the Destiny of the soul – have I preached on every
one of them in the past year?

Has my preaching had an evangelistic dimension? Have I,
perhaps, assumed too much about the Christian experience of
those who have been listening to me?

What are the fears most likely to be occupying their minds
at this time? Have I been on target in answering them?

These are questions about content, not about technique.
Later on we shall pose questions about the technical aspects of
preaching. For the moment, our focus is on our hearers, and
the consequent aims of our preaching. What ought to be
happening as a result?

So far we have been considering in broad terms the thought
processes that make up the preacher's 'piano practice'. Before
he ever gets into the pulpit, there are a number of important
things that have to happen in the privacy of his study. Our
thoughts have been focused on the character of preaching –
what it is, and what we hope to achieve by it. And it is right
that we should think of this first. For after all, without some
basis of approach, we can hardly get started.

But another question clamours for attention at this point. A
question, incidentally, that is foreign to other public professions, such as music and the theatre. It concerns the
character of the preacher.

No one asks that the professional musician or the actor
should be a paragon of virtue. In one sense, the question is
irrelevant to the question of his artistry. The actor may be a
rake, or a loving, concerned husband and father, since he
forsakes his real self and clothes himself in another character
on stage. The same applies to the concert pianist. When he
comes on to the concert platform, it is a matter of indifference
to the audience whether he slept in his own bed or someone
else's the night before. It is not a question they are likely to
ask. They only want to know whether or not his Beethoven or
his Chopin is beautiful. Again, the divorce between private
citizen and public man is absolute.

But the preacher is another matter entirely. Here any

contradiction between private life and public performance is
fatal to the integrity of the man.

Not that the preacher is perfect, or stands 'six feet above
contradiction'. The greatest Christian preacher of all time was
well aware that he was on a journey that was by no means
completed.

> Not that I have already obtained all this, or have already
> been made perfect, but I press on to take hold of that for
> which Christ Jesus took hold of me.
>
> Philippians 3:12

The best of us is an amalgam of good and evil, of sinner and
saint, and subject to temptation like the rest of mankind. The
preacher knows defeat as well as victory, and our hearers will
know it.

Nevertheless, one requirement of the preacher stands out
above all else. He needs to be someone alive to God, and
himself a pilgrim of eternity. Only on that basis can he point
others to the wicket-gate that marks the entry to the path of
life. His own experience of God's grace in Jesus Christ is the
only guarantee of having anything worth saying to others, and
the only warrant for standing in a pulpit to proclaim God's
Word. Said Gregory the Great, 'The hand that means to make
another clean, must not itself be dirty.' Certainly the preacher
must measure up to the Pauline standard of being 'above
reproach' as far as can be seen, in family life, in his conduct
and his ambitions (see 1 Timothy 2:1–7).

It is not necessary to spend much time discussing what is
meant by the call to preach. If we believe that God has called
us to the full-time ministry of preaching, then we would do
well to read Spurgeon's chapter on that subject in his *Lectures
to my Students* ('The call to the ministry' in the first series,
Lecture 2). There will be others who preach who are not full-
time ministers. They also need to have good grounds for
believing that God has given them the gifts and the calling to
preach.

But whether preaching is our life or only a part of it, the
basic requirements are much the same: a clear conviction
about our experience of Christ as Saviour, and an awareness

of our growth in grace and the knowledge of God. We should be experiencing in our own life what Paul prayed for his converts.

> For this reason I kneel before the Father, from whom his whole family in heaven and on earth derives its name. I pray that out of his glorious riches he may strengthen you with power through his Spirit in your inner being, so that Christ may dwell in your hearts through faith. And I pray that you, being rooted and established in love, may have power, together with all the saints, to grasp how wide and long and high and deep is the love of Christ, and to know this love that surpasses knowledge – that you may be filled to the measure of all the fullness of God.
>
> Ephesians 3:14-19

2

Choosing a theme

The concert pianist has one great advantage over the preacher when it comes to building a programme. The concert performer can repeat various items in his programmes dozens of times, since he is normally playing to a different audience each time he appears. The preacher usually has a much greater problem: he must change his theme every week, and produce new programmes.

However the analogy is not quite true. For the concert pianist would hardly be complete without certain staple items – a Beethoven sonata, some Chopin pieces, some dazzling encores which displayed his bravura skills. Sometimes, of course, the performer will devote a whole programme to one composer, or a whole series of concerts to a giant exercise – the complete cycle of Beethoven sonatas, for example. But this is abnormal, rather than normal.

A preacher is unlikely to preach the same sermon twice to the same congregation – at least within a year. (How many congregations would notice if the same sermon was preached twice in one year?) But he has the task of trying to build a balanced 'programme' through the weeks and months. The Gospel has many facets, many implications. The Bible is a rich and inexhaustible mine, from which new and fresh treasures may be brought. In another sense, the Gospel is also marvellously simple, and the preacher has in it a diamond, clear and transparent,which he holds up and turns each time he preaches so as to display a new facet of God's grace.

The problem, however, remains. The incessant need for the average pastor to have two messages a week, with only an occasional release from the demand for fresh messages, becomes for some men little less than torture, a task-master from whose

ceaseless demands there is no escape. Certainly, there are few
preachers who have sustained a continuous ministry in one
church for any length of time who have not had that feeling.

But there is another side to this question. Sometimes the
demand for new material and new themes seems like a great
cloud hanging over us, threatening and lowering. Clouds
bring rain! We also need the fresh mental attitude which
remembers that the Bible *does* have inexhaustible riches, and
that one can never preach on more than a fraction of the texts
and themes found in it. If every preacher has had those lean
periods of dryness, and seems to scratch around for a text,
living from hand to mouth, there are also other times when
texts and sermons seem to leap from the page with the clamant
demand, 'Preach on me! Preach on me!'

We must have a system to capture these moments, before the
inspiration runs away and the future harvest is lost. Joseph
storing up the abundance of the fruitful years against the lean
years is a type of the diligent preacher.

From the very start, the young preacher should have a place
to store sermon ideas. A loose-leaf notebook, or cards (6 x 4
inches are preferable to 5 x 3) that can be arranged in order are
best. During your regular reading, when ideas strike and
sometimes virtually complete outlines spring to mind from
the page, write them down. If you cannot use them immediately
then they will be preserved for future reference. Give no
thought to putting ideas into order, unless they shape themselves instinctively. The time for further work is when you
actually come to look at them again.

Choosing a text

Every sermon should start with a text, though we ought to
pause to ask, What is a text? Commonly, the preacher starts his
sermon by saying, 'My text today is from. . .' He then reads a
verse, and begins from there. However, this is to limit the use
of the word 'text' unnecessarily. The original meaning of 'text'
is from a Latin word meaning 'to weave' (compare our word
'textile'). 'A text is a passage of inspiration, which is woven
into the web of Holy Writ, and secondarily, into the web of a
discourse' (W.G.T. Shedd.) A text, then, is whatever part of

Scripture the sermon is based on. It may be part of a verse, a complete verse, several verses, a paragraph, a chapter – even a complete book of the Bible. (An excellent series of sermons could be based on the twelve Minor Prophets, taking one book per sermon.) When most congregations today seem ignorant of the sweep of biblical truth, it is important that we take large tracts of Scripture and give a bird's-eye view of them. There is great value in trying to encompass the message of a book in one sermon – even large books like Genesis, Jeremiah, Revelation, or one of the Gospels. More often, more likely, we shall want to concentrate on smaller segments. Almost any verse from the Pauline epistles will provide ample material for a whole sermon. One of the parables or miracles of Jesus is adequate for a message. Many of the sayings of Jesus demand careful and detailed exposition, and require a whole sermon for their treatment.

It should hardly be necessary to recommend the practice of expository preaching; by which we mean, diligently working through a whole book of the Bible on successive Sundays. Although it is worth noting that Spurgeon never used this particular method, it is nevertheless one which many notable preachers have used. (We might mention Martyn Lloyd-Jones and Alexander Maclaren as examples.) The value of the expository method is that it drives the preacher to tackle *everything* in a particular book, rather than hopping across difficult, obscure, or uncomfortable aspects of Scripture. Rather than using the stepping-stone method, we should wade through the river of Scripture. For example, when preaching through the Pastoral Epistles of Paul, we encounter passages which deal with qualifications of elders and deacons. Using the expository method, no one can accuse us of preaching 'at' any particular person or group of people in the church. At the same time, many will appreciate our wrestling with such chapters and tackling the problems they raise.

Of course, even this method used insensitively has its dangers. Spurgeon may have avoided this method simply because of one bad experience as a yound lad. Let him tell it in his own words:

I have a very lively, or rather a deadly, recollection of a certain series of discourses on the Hebrews, which made a deep impression on my mind of the most undesirable kind. I wished frequently that the Hebrews had kept the epistle to themselves for it sadly bored one poor Gentile lad. By the time the seventh or eighth discourse had been delivered, only the very good people could stand it; these of course, declared that they had never heard more valuable expositions, but to those of a more carnal judgement it appeared that each sermon increased in dullness.

C.H. Spurgeon, *Lectures* (1st series), p. 99.

We should be aware when our hearers are no longer listening enthusiastically, or are getting tired of a particular series – and have the courage to give such a series the *coup de grace*.

So what is so important about having a text? Why do we continue this practice of announcing the text, or passage, we are about to expound?

I think the first reason is that *it establishes our authority*. Preaching is different from every other form of public speech. The preacher's authority does not rest on the extent of his learning, the skill of his oratory, or even the ordination which has granted him the right to preach. He stands as the servant of the living God, bound by the Word of God, under whose authority he lives, and to which bar he brings all that he has to say. He does not claim infallibility; much less does he claim the right to govern and order the lives of his hearers by some personal right. But he does claim to bring a word from the Lord, a message from the Throne, an utterance which by the transforming power of the Spirit may become a communication of divine truth. The preacher is not a purveyor of opinions, or a peddlar of theories. At times he may be both of these, but the best preaching becomes the vehicle of a divine encounter, whereby God actually meets with those who are listening to his Word. As Campbell Morgan says,

My sermon has no authority in it at all, except as an interpretation or an exposition or an illustration of the truth which is in the text. The text is everything. That is the point of authority.

A second reason for announcing a text, and taking our stand upon it, is that *it defines and limits the message*. This means that the text gives us our subject. It really encapsulates all that we want to say, and gives dimensions to our discourse. In that sense it resembles the architect's plan. The preacher who has prayed over his choice of text, or believes that in the consecutive exposition of Scripture he has chosen the right segment for the congregation's attention, must seek to discover just what the text says, both in its eternal, changeless meaning and in its application to this particular time and place.

Let me urge as emphatically as possible that the apprentice preacher should take this aspect of our topic seriously. Just as there are no two exact synonymns, no two words which mean precisely the same thing, so there are no two texts of Scripture which say the same thing. Many are similar, many are parallel, many echo other passages, but each is distinct, individual and unique.

One method of preaching which is all too prevalent is to take the chosen text, and then to draw the congregation's attention to numerous passages elsewhere in the Bible which say something similar. The intention is usually to use parallel passages to illuminate the text. Too often the result is a tedious paper-chase through the Scriptures, whilst leaving the text itself unexplored, at least in depth. The preacher, as well as the long-suffering congregation, would have done better to stay with his text and to have turned over the soil there. That's where the treasure was all the time.

Why does this so often happen? The answer, I fear, is that some preachers are just not willing for the labour, the toil and the sweat involved in digging out the meaning of the text. They get tired and discouraged because the text doesn't expose enough ideas for a whole sermon quickly enough, and therefore don't persist in the effort.

This is not to say that word studies which trace the meaning of the great ideas of Scripture are not a legitimate method. When it is done properly it can be as exciting as a treasure hunt. But it is not this to which I am referring at this point. I am simply pointing out the danger of not treating the chosen text thoroughly.

The point about the text prescribing the limits of our

discourse lies just here. It is this text, we believe, that is to form the basis of the message. We need to worry it, just like a dog worries a bone, until it yields up its secret. Each word is important: the sentence structure, the grammar, the syntax, the thought pattern – all are intrinsic to the meaning. Of course, there are other important factors – the meaning of the text within the book, within the context, and in its multifaceted application to life. These will be dealt with elsewhere. But let me emphasise again: the text defines for us the shape and boundary of the message.

One thing more needs to be said about our choice of texts. Choose the big ones! By that I mean, the mighty utterances of Jesus, Paul and the prophets. They demand our attention. Sometimes they seem so profound and vast in their implications that the thought of trying to explain them, let alone of doing so successfully, is daunting. How much easier to leave them for the present and tackle them when we are more experienced and skilful. But we must nevertheless try to preach on these passages, even if we do not fully succeed. For example, there is no doubt in my mind that John 3:16 is probably the most difficult verse to preach on – simply because when you have read it you have said all that there is to be said about it. It is simple – a child can grasp its essential truth. But it is also so profound that the greatest intellect cannot get round it. When I have read it, there is nothing more I can say. But what tragedy if we never preach on it.

A man should begin early to grapple with great subjects, therefore he should seek for great texts. As the athlete gains might by great exertions, so a man does not overstrain his powers by taking great texts. The more he wrestles, the more he will gain strength. He must not merely dream over the subject or play with it. The things that agitate the world, the things that agitate your own bosoms – preach on them. The things we would like to have settled before we die – settle them and preach on them. The things you would ask an apostle if you had the chance to talk to him – get your Bible and preach on them.

G.C. Morgan *Preaching*, p. 74.

Choosing a theme – choosing an interpretation

Before we proceed to deal with the actual process by which a text is turned into a sermon, there is one more preliminary question that needs to be dealt with. That concerns the basic approach of all texts. For before the man stands in the pulpit as a preacher, he sits in the study as an interpreter.

To begin with, every preacher starts out with certain basic convictions, which become in due course his assumptions. His view of the Bible as a whole is of immense importance. His view of the inspiration of Scripture will profoundly influence his approach to *any* text. His understanding of biblical language will undoubtedly have some bearing on his competence as an interpreter and subsequently as an expositor. If he subscribes to a particular system of interpretation (e.g. premillenial, typological, dispensational, or whatever), this will govern his approach to a particular passage. His theology, whether Calvinist, Arminian, Barthian, or something else will also tend to be a filter through which the text is passed. In other words, all that influences the way we deal with a text is part of the basic programme which has been built in to our minds.

On another level, the preacher's view of life will also affect his interpretation. He may be a man of wide learning and broad culture, with a profound knowledge of literature and the arts. Such a person may lack the common touch and the ability to relate to people. He lives in the rarefied atmosphere of books and ideas. On the other hand, another man may delight in the world of affairs, wanting nothing more than to meet people, to spend time with them, whether on the golf course, in the Rotary Club or in their homes. He would far rather spend time in the garden than in his study, or take a stroll with the dog than sit down with a book. This is little more than to say that each of us is different, and we tend to fall into certain moulds of temperament and type. Nevertheless, the kind of person we are is going to affect our approach to a passage of Scripture. What we need is to be aware of this, and to try to compensate for our weaknesses, as well as draw upon our strengths.

All this may seem commonplace and obvious. It is merely saying that we bring to our sermonising certain assumptions and certain personalities, and these affect the way we look at

the text of Scriptures. The point to notice, however, is that we
are so often unaware of it. All our assumptions and pre-
suppositions tend to get in the way of our view of the text. We
speak to *it*, rather than letting *it* speak to us. The preacher
who never stands back and looks at himself critically is in
danger of becoming his own worst enemy. To realise that you
bring certain mental baggage to any text of Scripture is an
asset in dealing with it. It makes you freer to hear what the text
is saying, and enables it to speak more clearly. It may enable us
to see something in the text that we might have missed, simply
because we had been thinking along certain well-worn tracks.
It seems to me that one of the preacher's greatest temptations,
especially for the man who has been preaching for a good
number of years, is to approach the text of Scripture in the
same way as he did last week, last month, last year. Simply
because he has become accustomed to looking for a certain
structure, a familiar pattern, a pattern that 'fits', there is the
danger of his preaching becoming dull and uniform. The
explosive, disconcerting character of the Bible will slip by him
and make him unable to be struck afresh, even shattered, by its
message. The Word of the Lord is no longer a fire, or a
hammer that breaks the rock in pieces (Jeremiah 23:29), but
rather like a comfort blanket or an old friend that we meet on
the way to work every morning to whom we tip our hat as we
pass.

The preacher then is an *interpreter*. Some guidance for
interpreting Scripture is necessary. This is not a book on
hermeneutics, but the preacher should from time to time be
aware of the issues which are exercising biblical scholars. He
will need to master the contents of the Bible, and to become
skilful in discerning patterns, themes, and threads of Scripture.
The thought has been finely put by John Ker:

> The great work of the Christian preacher is not to be an
> orator, but an interpreter, to teach the people how to read
> and use the Word of God. He is a conveyance-pipe to draw
> the water from the fountain and pour it on the grass and
> flowers to make them grow, also on consuming fires of sin
> to extinguish them. But for this he must know where to
> draw from, and what to pour it upon; whether as the small

rain on the tender herb, or with the overpowering gush. There are preachers who invert the right treatment, who are hard with the weak and weak with the hard. Notice how Christ varies his treatment as He deals with proud Pharisees or repentant sinners.

3

Shaping the structure

Every musician, whether professional or the merest amateur, has pondered the mysterious process whereby a page covered with dots can be transformed into ravishing sound. And any musician will readily concede that those pages of printed notes are only the starting point of a performance. First the pianist, violinist or whoever must get those notes 'under his hands', as they say, so that he can play them correctly. That is akin to the preacher doing his homework in the basic task of interpretation, ensuring that at least he understands the biblical text.

For there is all the difference in the world between simply playing all the notes correctly, and a performance by a master musician. Even performances by great exponents of the composer may differ quite markedly, whilst both may be true to the musical text. Both will reveal different aspects of the written notes, but their distinct musical personalities will emerge in the way they interpret the piece of music.

The same is true of preachers and preaching. Each preacher starts from the biblical text. But beyond that, sermons are as diverse as preachers themselves. The way they shape their material, their treatment of the theme, the way in which their personality comes across in their sermons – these are extremely diverse.

According to the old adage, 'preachers are born, not made'. Properly understood, this is undoubtedly true. The ability to preach, or at least the raw gift of preaching, is something which is *given*. Musical genius, much discussed yet never wholly fathomed, is much the same. There is no way to account for a Mozart, a Liszt, a Schubert. Great pianists are also born rather than made.

Yet this is only part of the story. There has never been a great performer who has not also been immensely diligent in developing the divine gift. Gifts are the starting point, not the final word in performance.

One can believe firmly in the gift of preaching, but one will study the history of homiletics in vain for a preacher who became famous and mightily used by God who was not also a labourer. In other words there is a gift of preaching, and blessed is the man who has that to begin with. Perhaps one could hardly become a *great* preacher without it. But there is also a craft, and that can be learnt, with sufficient determination and perspiration.

Looked at from another point of view, one might suggest that it is up to us to prepare our sermons by hard work, and then to seek from the Lord the added dimension of spiritual power which will make them effective. Spurgeon has a lecture entitled 'The Holy Spirit in connection with our ministry' (Spurgeon [1877], Lecture I). The whole lecture is worth reading, but this much may be quoted, from page 3:

> To us, as ministers, the Holy Spirit is absolutely essential. . .
> If we have not the Spirit which Jesus promised, we cannot
> perform the commission which Jesus gave.

Now let us examine the whole process of shaping the structure in more detail. We have our chosen passage before us. What should we do to deal with it homiletically?

This is not the time to reach for commentaries. Even if we are dealing with a passage which we feel has exegetical problems, or which is going to be difficult to interpret correctly, we should resist the temptation to reach for help from our book shelves at this moment. We are preachers, not lecturers, and we want the text to speak, and to write its own message upon a clean slate. The lecturer ought not to make a scholarly gaffe, but his purpose is distinctly different from the preacher's. The preacher ought not to make a scholarly gaffe either, but he can check that later. For the time being, let's hold off consulting anything other than our own instincts, our mind's perception, and a prayerful dependence upon the Spirit's illumination. This was also the view of Campbell Morgan, prince of early twentieth century preachers:

Two things are vital, first personal first-hand work on the text, and then all scholarly aids available. I never take down a commentary until I have done the first-hand work and made my outline. To turn to commentaries first is to create a second-hand mentality. I speak freely from a most carefully prepared brief.

H. Murray, *Campbell Morgan, Bible teacher.*

In a word, a text requires meditation for it to disclose its inmost secret. And such a process takes time and effort.

A sermon that has not fermented in the vat of its author's struggle, imagination, and interpretation is underprepared no matter how many hours were clocked on it. In a word, preachers have a tendency to depend too obsessively and too long on commentaries and secondary materials and to brood and imagine too fearfully and too little about what way a text or subject is trying to have with them . . . There is no mystery here and no magic. Nor is there any license for slipshod and neglectful preparation. Instead, there is an affirmation of the central importance of the preacher's creative encounter and struggle with a text as the nursery of faithful preaching. (Nichols)

We are going to delay talking about the introduction until later. The introduction is never our first concern. It is better left until we raise the whole question of how to begin and end a sermon. Our first concern here is to give some help with viewing the text homiletically, that is, with a view to making a sermon from it.

We have before us a number of words of Scripture, either more or less. If we have a single verse or a longer passage the approach will be slightly different in each case, but not greatly.

The best way to proceed now is to take some examples. (The reader will find it helpful to have the Bible open at the appropriate place.)

Example 1 Philippians 4:6–7

Do not be anxious about anything, but in everything, by prayer and petition, with thanksgiving, present your requests to God, and the peace of God, which transcends all understanding, will guard your hearts and your minds in Christ Jesus.

We begin by asking some questions. The answers can be scribbled down on a sheet of paper, preferably A4. At this stage we are not much concerned with order, only with allowing the text to speak.

1. What is the main idea which seems to speak in these verses? Underline what you think are the key words. (*You may wish to cover up the next part of the page while you write your choice of key words.*)

Some of the key words are: *anxious*; *prayer, petition and thanksgiving* (we could circle them together and label it *prayer*); *peace*; *guard*.

2. Do these words suggest any sort of plan? Can you see any way to group the ideas they suggest to us? Do you find two, three, four or more main ideas here? Read the verses again and again until you begin to discern some pattern and shape to the passage.

What has emerged from your first pondering of the text? Probably three basic ideas: anxiety; prayer; peace. We need to bring these words back to the text, looking at them in the framework of the text as a whole, and ponder them again.

3. Our next question is this: can we produce statements which reveal the meaning of these words *in their setting*? This last qualification is very important. We could make literally hundreds of statements about each of them apart from their context here in Philippians. For example, we could immediately think of plenty of things to say about prayer. But we must be careful to restrict ourselves to seeing prayer in relation to these verses only.

Let's try to make some statements. Remember that we are thinking aloud, and scribbling our thoughts down without too much thought of order at this stage.

Thinking about the first section of verse 6, let's put down

the following statement (remembering that this is a tentative process, open to modification later on – sometimes abandoned altogether, or re-thought completely):

The anxiety which threatens our serenity. What does Paul recommend as the response to that anxiety which is so prevalent in our lives? The short answer is: prayer. He qualifies it as 'prayer and petition, with thanksgiving ... requests to God'. Can we make a statement about that which will link it with what precedes it? As I pondered these various expressions which Paul uses about prayer, it occurred to me that really he is suggesting a certain *attitude*, a response to life's problems. Prayer is more than speaking, more than its constituent parts. It is a turning to God in faith and trust. Can we make a statement about that? I believe we can. What about:

The attitude which expresses our faith. Then comes Paul's magnificent expression which is such a precious treasure, and has been to the people of God in every age. 'And the peace of God which transcends [I think I prefer the older translation "passes"] all understanding, will guard [or keep] your hearts and minds in Christ Jesus.' This is such a comprehensive statement that we may well find it difficult to find words which capture the fullness of meaning. Perhaps this is the point at which to say that we are looking for statements which will become the headings and divisions of our sermon, the bones of the skeleton. We shall have plenty to say when we come to fill out each section with flesh. Just now we are looking for a brief statement to put alongside the others we have.

I recall that the word translated 'guard' or 'keep' in verse 7 has the meaning in the original Greek of a 'bastion', part of the strongest defence of a castle. If you have any knowledge of Greek, then check this in the Greek New Testament, and then look up this word in a lexicon. It may be suggestive later on. (It also comes to mind that the start of the French Revolution stemmed from an event called 'The storming of the Bastille', a notorious prison in Paris. There are certain overwhelming threats to our peace and assurance which comes to all of us in the course of life which could well be illustrated by a reference to the Storming of the Bastille.) We make a note of this in case we wish to use it later. Reminder: pour out all such thoughts on paper at this stage. Don't worry if they might not be used.

We want to open our mind to every prompting of memory, imagination and illustration.

Incidentally, the third or fourth heading in a sermon outline often causes us the most mental toil. It is often hard to find words which 'fit' with the other headings. But let's make an attempt, even if we have to alter it later on.

The peace which enfolds our life. I want to improve on that. But as I've racked my brains and turned it this way and that, it hasn't yielded up its secret yet. Perhaps it will; maybe it won't. Much will depend upon the time we have for preparation. If the week has been rushing by and this sermon is for next Sunday I may have to live with a compromise, and use a heading that is not perfect. After all, ultimately it is the substance of the sermon which is the most important thing, not the headings. The headings are important because they provide the structure which tends to guide my thoughts in working on the sermon content. If the sermon is not needed immediately, it will be possible to come back to my headings, and look at them again with a view to improving them.

So, we have a rough outline, consisting of three headings.
1.   The anxiety which threatens our serenity.
2.   The attitude which expresses our faith.
3.   The peace which enfolds our life.

Before proceeding further, we need to comment on some other matters which enter the picture here.

One concerns the unity of the sermon. When we break down a passage of scripture for the purposes of preaching a sermon, or treating it homiletically, we can sometimes finish up with three or four diverse statements which have no connection with each other. The danger then is that we shall preach 'sermonettes' which lack unity, and therefore do not really make a sermon.

Looking again at this passage in Philippians, we see that there is a problem which Paul raises – the problem of anxiety. Next he points to the response we make to the threat of anxiety, namely, prayer and trust. We turn to God in our need. Thirdly, he suggests what God's response to our attitude of faith will be – the provision of peace which will ensure we will have adequate defence amidst the storms of life. There is an underlying unity of theme here which ought to emerge in our structure so that we make one comprehensive statement about a particular issue in the Christian life on the basis of Paul's words.

A second matter concerns the way in which we frame our headings. It has always seemed to me that it is highly desirable to try and find headings which express a complete thought, rather than simply to use a few words. For example, it might be thought that we could use for our headings the three words, 1. Anxiety; 2. Prayer; 3. Peace.

Now the whole purpose of a sermon outline is that it tries to encompass the meaning of the passage of Scripture we have chosen for the sermon. As we have suggested, each passage of Scripture is unique, and that uniqueness ought to be discovered and preserved by the preacher. It is obvious that single words could be written over hundreds of different passages – you only have to look in a concordance to see that there are a multitude of passages which make reference, for example, to peace. We are suggesting that an outline seeks to comprehend this passage (and no other) in a series of statements. That is why we spend time trying to encompass the thoughts expressed in the verses of our text in short statements.

Another matter which calls for comment concerns the use of alliteration, which the dictionary defines as 'the commencing of two or more words in close connection with the same letter or sound'. It is a literary device common in poetry, e.g. 'In a summer season when soft was the sun.' The use of alliteration by the preacher is meant to make his headings more memorable. After all, one of the main reasons for having headings at all is to seek to convey the main outline of the sermon to the congregation in such a way that they can remember it.

In the outline we produce from Philippians 3:6,7 there was a possibility of alliteration. The first heading used the words, *The Anxiety which threatens our serenity*. The second also used an A in the keyword: *The Attitude which expresses our faith*. When it came to the third heading, the preacher who is sold on alliteration would have scratched his head to find another word starting with A. He might have come up with something like *The Armour which protects our life* or *The Appropriation of God's peace*; or *The Answer to the storms of life*. None of these seems to me to provide an adequate substitute for the key word *peace* which we actually chose. Alliteration can be helpful, but it should never become our master, or it will lead us to mistreat Scripture.

Some preachers are much more skilled in the use of alliteration than others. Some undoubtedly take it to extreme lengths, not only using alliteration in the main headings but in the sub-headings as well. As an example of what we mean, take a look at these two outlines by preachers who have always been renowned for their use of alliteration.

The first is by George B. Duncan, and is on the text 'The people . . . found grace in the wilderness', from Jeremiah 31:2.

1. *A place that was desolate*
     It was a place of dreariness
     It was a place of death
     It was a place of danger
2. *A path that was dreaded*
     The loneliness of the way
     The hardness of the way
     The emptiness of the way
3. *A provision that was discovered*
     A daily provision
     A divine presence
     A definite purpose

The second example is by Stephen Olford, and was a message preached at the Keswick Convention in 1959, where he has been a regular speaker for many years. It is based on the familiar text in Galatians 2:20, 'Christ liveth in me'.

1. *The miracle of Christ's indwelling*
     He indwells by a miraculous operation
     He indwells by a miraculous revelation
2. *The measure of his indwelling*
3. *The mastery of Christ's indwelling*
     That we may know the mastery of indwelling victory
     That we may know the mastery of indwelling purity
     That we may know the mastery of indwelling energy

It is not altogether fair to give just an outline in this way, since so much depends upon other factors, such as the way the preacher fills out his material, his presentation, and his overall impact – something that is not easily conveyed in cold print! But it is not difficult to see pitfalls in such preaching. Sometimes such a consistent use of alliteration impresses us with the preacher's cleverness or skill with words, rather than helping us to form a proper idea of the passage being expounded. As one preacher said to me, 'The problem with excessive alliteration is that any crossword addicts in the congregation will soon find themselves anticipating the findings of the preacher by many minutes and indeed ending with five points for his three – instead of listening to the Word of God they (and the preacher too) are playing word games.'

Another point of discussion raised by our treatment of this passage from Philippians concerns the number of headings to use in a sermon.

We chose three, and did so because it seemed that the passage fell quite naturally into three separate sections, each encompassing a distinct thought in Paul's words. When we set out to treat a passage homiletically, we do not start with the assumption that there is going to be a three-fold, four-fold or any other division of the text. We must always be guided by the natural sense and structure of the passage we are dealing with.

It is undoubtedly true that multitudes of sermons fall into three sections, and multitudes of preachers almost invariably try and use three-point sermons. For example, it is said of Alexander Maclaren, a renowned Baptist preacher of the late 19th century, that he had a silver hammer which he used to strike any text, and it fell apart naturally into three heads. If we examine his sermons, we shall find this to be the case.

Text: But ye have not so learned Christ; if so be that ye
                    have heard him, and have been taught by
                    him.

                                         Ephesians 4:20,21

1.   *The living voice of Christ himself is our teacher*
2.   *Those who are in Christ receive continuous instruction*
               from Him
3.   *The theme of the teaching is the Teacher*

F.W. Robertson, who is still regarded as pre-eminent among Anglican preachers of the 19th century, and particularly as a stylist, tended to use a two-fold structure. For example, on John 17:19 his headings are

1. The sanctification of Jesus Christ;
2. The sanctification of his people

In another memorable sermon, entitled 'The irreparable past', preached in 1853 on Mark 14:41,42, the two sections of the sermon are simply;

1. The irreparable past
2. The available future

C.H. Spurgeon, the incomparable giant, was much more diverse in the number of sections within any given sermon. His headings vary between two and ten!

In one sense, the number of headings is unimportant. What *is* important is that the headings should encompass the meaning of the text, bringing out the truths that are there. Whether two, three, four, or more will depend, first, upon the demands of the text (i.e. our choice and working must be exegetically controlled), and second, upon the requirements of the situation (how long we have available to preach, how long each section will take to deal with, and so on). One thing is certain: it is better to preach two sermons on the same text, than to labour through a sermon beyond the capacity of the congregation to bear it. What was appropriate to the Puritan age, with its three or four hour sermons, is totally inappropriate to the demands of the congregation in a television age, which conditions people to communication in small segments, rather than in large chunks.

To sum up, we should make sure that our headings, whether few or many, really are the best possible treatment of the chosen text.

The question may be asked, Can we not abandon headings altogether? Why not simply preach the sermon in one piece, without the artificiality of divisions? In a basic treatment like this, this is too large a matter to deal with in depth. My opinion is that most preachers and most congregations need

them! Too many sermons I hear lack structure, rather than
having too much. A strong body needs a firm skeleton. Of
course, the bones do not have to stick out, but they should be
there, supported by the flesh. I call as a witness the American
Paul Scherer, well known as a great preacher as well as a
teacher of homiletics. In his book *For We Have This Treasure*
he wrote:

> After you have determined what emphasis your subject and
> material call for, it is then that you begin to organize your
> thought under heads. And I am definitely of the opinion
> that it is well for the structure to show. There is no painting
> of the human figure without some knowledge of human
> anatomy; and unless the framework is manifest to a degree,
> what you have is no longer human. It is either surrealism or
> it is a jelly-fish. I have listened to sermons that without aim
> did 'go round', as Browning has it, 'in an eddy of
> purposeless dust, effort unending and vain'. You are to have
> a framework – and let it show.

In the next chapter, we shall be concerned about how that
flesh is created. Here we are far more concerned with
foundations, the basic structure, and the outline.

At this point, we want to make another attempt to show the
working of our method in shaping the structure. Our first
example was only two verses long, a brief extract from
Philippians. It will be helpful now to try and tackle a much
longer passage. Not forgetting, of course, that our definition
of a 'text' is the total segment of Scripture that we propose to
expound in a sermon. Sometimes, we put a few words under
the microscope; at other times, it is good to go up in an
aeroplane and look at the whole landscape. Both ways of
looking at Scripture are important and helpful.

An Old Testament passage

We move on from a text in the New Testament, where the
sermon was based on a single verse, to a much longer passage
in the Old Testament. Once again, I suggest you turn to the
passage, so that it may be in front of you as we seek to

construct a sermon from it. It is from the book of Isaiah, chapter 55. It is important to read it several times before we begin to work on it, so that we may get the general meaning and shape of the passage. Then we are ready to start thinking about how to approach it sermonically.

What springs to mind as we read it again? Here are some thoughts that might occur to us:

- It is all about God's feast.
- The invitation in verse 1 brings Jesus' invitation in Matthew 11:28 to mind.
- God's gifts here are all free.
- The whole passage brings thoughts of the Lord's Supper to mind. This is particularly seen in the reference to 'covenant' in v. 3.
- The chapter is all written as the utterance of God, that is to say, God is the speaker throughout. (That may be important in terms of the emphasis we make in our sermon.)
- There is a huge contrast between the lavish bounty of God and the poverty of those who are invited.

Now as we ponder some of these facts we are ready to make the next move. And that is to try and shape the passage into building blocks so that we can move towards a sermon. (Once again, as we suggested in dealing with the Philippians passage, the reader is urged to lay this textbook aside so that he may concentrate and work on Isaiah 55 for himself.)

The thought that keeps coming to mind is that of a rich feast such as might have been prepared by a rich Eastern merchant for his guests. Only here God is the host. Trying to express that as simply as possible, we come up with this idea: *The feast that God has prepared.* How we proceed to expand that thought need not concern us overmuch now, but it is not too difficult to see some of the elements in the passage which will be pointers. There is the contrast between going out to dinner (which may cost us a packet), or going to a wedding (likewise expensive), with the thought here of God's bounty which is provided for the thirsty and hungry *freely.* And as soon as that thought comes to mind, we begin to remember the

contrast between the man who determines to pay for his
salvation through works, prayers, religion or whatever, and
the free gift of salvation which comes through Jesus Christ.
How amazing to be the guest of God. By his grace, God invites
us to enjoy the riches which are found in his Son, the Lord
Jesus Christ. And in keeping with the whole idea of God
sending his Son is the thought of God actually seeking
fellowship with men, rather than waiting for them to seek
him. And that surely is the emphasis here in Isaiah 55.

The next heading is suggested by verses 3-5 where the key
word is clearly 'convenant'. The word is full of significance in
the OT. The covenants with Noah, with Abraham, and with
the Children of Israel at Sinai will immediately spring to
mind. But Isaiah 55 speaks of an 'everlasting' covenant, which
contrasts with previous OT covenants. Of course, if our minds
keep hold of the thought of the Lord's Supper, we shall be
instantly reminded that Jesus inaugurated the New Convenant
in his blood in the upper room. We need not doubt that what
God spoke to Isaiah some eight centuries before Christ refers
to that New Covenant. And through the long centuries, God
was faithfully working out his purposes to bring that covenant
based on 'my unfailing kindnesses to David' to pass. The
thought has emerged to give us our second heading: *The
faithfulness that God has promised.* I should want to develop
this segment of the sermon along a number of possible lines.
Besides the comparisons between the Old and New Covenants,
I would want to show people something of God's faithfulness
today, and remind them that the succeeding verses speak of
Jesus' gathering of many peoples. 'And I, when I be lifted up
from the earth will draw all men to myself' (John 12:32).

Returning to Isaiah, verses 6 and 7 are something of a
contrast. They bring to our attention that though God's feast
is free, and available to all, it is not cheap. It demands a
seriousness from those who want to avail themselves of the
rich blessings of God. It involves a turning from sin, and a
turning to God in faith. This need not surprise us, since this is
a basic message of the whole Bible. And if we are preaching at
the celebration of the Lord's Supper, then a reminder of our
need to be right with God (and men) will be entirely fitting.
Yet the thought of God's free bounty is uppermost even here.

This is expressed in the words, 'he will freely pardon' which may give us a clue to our next heading. What about *A forgiveness that God provides*?

The marvellous thing about God's forgiveness is that it is priceless, and yet free. Nevertheless it is conditional – in the same way that the marriage vows are conditional. The bride and bridegroom speak of 'forsaking all others' as well as being faithful to each other as long as they live. The thought will naturally lead us back to the Lord's Table, to the humble receiving of God's forgiveness by means of the blood of Christ, and the receiving too of all the riches which come to us through our union with him.

Perhaps we have enough for a sermon already. It would, of course, be possible to continue in the following verses to explore more of the promises of God. The faithfulness of God in the sending of his Word (vv. 8-11) and the joy and gladness which are promised as a result (vv, 12,13) are wonderfully set forth here.

A fitting thought with which to conclude is found in the *New Bible Commentary Revised* (1970) on Isaiah 55: 'This call to the needy is unsurpassed for warmth of welcome even in the NT.' If I were preaching on this passage, I might well conclude with further references to the invitations of Jesus to 'Come' (we referred to Matthew 11:28 above), reinforcing the invitation of God in Isaiah with the words of the Saviour himself.

A word of comment about preaching from the OT might be helpful here. I think we need have no hesitation about preaching from the OT Christologically. After all, this is precisely what the early Christian preachers did, as the sermons in Acts and the epistles make abundantly evident. The Church has always believed that the Bible is one – unified in the God of whom it speaks, and therefore Trinitarian, and unified too in the salvation it proclaims. As we have seen, a passage like Isaiah 55 would lose so much if we failed to link it with the New Covenant, and it lends itself without strain to a Communion message. It is full of the Gospel, and so is all the Old Testament if we read it with the eyes of faith.

Telling the Story

So far, we have been concerned primarily with sermons based on a text and a chapter. Much of our preaching will be of that kind, using the statements of Scripture as the basis of preaching that explains the meaning of biblical truth. We need not apologise for believing in preaching that has strong doctrinal content, and seeks to order the revelation of Scripture in terms of propositions.

But a moment's reflection will remind us that great tracts of the Bible are stories. The Bible is God's story, a story that began in the Garden of Eden and will only be completed in the other Garden that is described in the book of Revelation. In between we have the stories of the Patriarchs (Abraham, Isaac, Jacob), the Children of Israel (from the Exodus right through the kings up to and including the Exile), the greatest story of all in the life, death and resurrection of Jesus Christ, and the story of the Church (told in Acts and Epistles), climaxing in that marvellous picture book, the Revelations of St John.

Now we are obviously using 'story' in a special way. Somewhat ambiguously, you may feel. After all, we use the word 'story' in many different ways in everyday speech. We talk about 'a short story', when we mean a made-up story, a piece of fiction. And we also talk about 'a news story' when we mean a record of events, basically factual, that really happened. We also talk about 'a story I heard the other day' which may be a piece of gossip, or the kind of story a comedian tells, or a piece of news that we were told which was about real people and real events.

The Bible is full of stories, short and long. There are the stories that Jesus told, and the stories told about the things that Jesus said and did. There are the stories from the Old Testament, such as those from the time of the Judges or the Prophets, and there are the stories which tell of the adventures of the first Christians, and the Apostle Paul. To put it in another way, the Bible consists of history, biography, parable, autobiography and fables. And there is also the over-arching story which runs like a thread through both Testaments, the story of redemption. The story of how God prepared for the coming of the Redeemer, and how he actually came, and the results of his coming.

Now the preacher has this great fund of stories at his disposal, and he would be foolish not to use it. First of all, simply by telling the stories themselves. In these days of widespread ignorance of Scripture, there is surely great value in telling the Bible stories more or less as straight narratives. The man who takes the trouble to master the story of the Flood, the stories of Jacob, Saul, David, Ruth and so on, will always have an appreciative audience. For every grown-up loves a story as much as every child. Jesus knew this, and capitalised on it in his teaching, which is full of stories. We call them parables, which is simply to say that they are stories told for the purpose of explaining heavenly truth by means of earthly incidents. And what wonderful stories they are – the Prodigal Son, the Wise and Foolish Virgins, the Pharisee and the Publican, the Sower and so on. And then there are the stories of Jesus' miracles – Jairus' daughter, changing water into wine at Cana, the man let down through the roof, the stilling of the storm on the Lake of Galilee and the raising of Lazarus.

So we could go on, but we have said enough to show how broad is the concept of 'story' in the Bible, and how readily it lends itself to the skill of the preacher. The next step is to use an example of a Bible story as the basis of a sermon. Now the obvious difficulty in trying to explain how such a sermon 'works' is that we cannot tell the story in the way we would do so in the pulpit. The essence of a 'story-sermon' is the telling of the story, and apart from printing out the entire sermon, much of the impact of the sermon is lost. All we can hope to do is to show *how to approach* the particular story and how we might tackle it.

The first example is taken from Mark 5:24–34, the story of the woman who came and touched Jesus' robe. This is, you remember, a story within a story, for it comes in the narrative of the healing of Jairus' daughter. As Jesus was on the way to Jairus' house, the un-named woman stole up behind Jesus, touched his garment and was healed. The point of the story is that it illustrates what happens when someone comes to Jesus. Mark first of all paints a vivid picture of her condition, and the uselessness of all the cures she tried; the endless traipsing round from one doctor to another, each one promising success, and each one failing to help her. It is a sad and sorry picture. But it is no less pathetic than the way in which so many people look for happiness to help them with their problems, and seem to turn in every direction before they seek for God's answer. A little imagination will enable us to compare the two situations – that of the woman, and that of people today. And the more vivid we can make the narrative the better. I would suggest here the value of some of the books which describe life in the lands of the Bible. (A good example is *Everyday life in the Holy Land* by James Neil.)

It is significant that this woman would have been excluded from the Temple worship, and thus by implication from fellowship with God. Then if we look beneath the surface we can discover various hindrances to her coming to Jesus for help; hindrances which again can without too much effort be compared to those encountered even now. But despite all the obstacles she exercised her faith, and in six steps we can show how she (and countless multitudes since) came to Jesus. She came; she touched; she believed; she felt; she fell at his feet; and she told him the whole truth. Again, all these steps need illustrating and applying to make them come alive to the congregation before us. We shall also want to press home several other points, particularly about the wonderful *power* of Jesus; the *freedom* that Jesus promised (see v. 34); and the *peace* that he gave (also v. 34).

It is not difficult to see the value of this story for the preacher. First of all, it enables us to show the power of Jesus, and to focus on his healing touch. Secondly, we are able to use the story to explain the way of salvation in an actual example, and to do so simply without the use of difficult theological concepts. And thirdly, it is a story that speaks quite readily to the life-situation of people today. It is easy to draw parallels between the position of so many people today, and the woman with the crippling disease who came falteringly to Jesus and received his healing touch.

Many stories from the Bible can be treated in this way, and whole series of useful preaching can be built upon biographies of biblical characters. Similarly, the great historical incidents like the Exodus, the Desert Wanderings, the Kingdoms, the Exile and Return, lend themselves equally readily to preaching.

My second example is taken from the life of King Saul. The record of the life of King Saul reminds us that many of the stories of the Bible are by way of warning. To mention the names of Lot, Samson, Absolom, and Ananias and Sapphira is to be reminded that the Bible records folly and failure and faith and success in equal measure. So in our preaching we need to deal with examples of both. In fact, people probably find it easier to identify with the weaknesses and failures of some biblical characters than with the spiritual giants that we often set before them as models. Both Jesus and Paul used examples from the Old Testament to warn their hearers.

I often find it useful, even when telling the story of a biblical character whose life story occupies several chapters, to try and find a verse which characterises the story as a whole, or epitomises the individual's life. So in the case of Saul a good verse to choose is 1 Samuel 26:21. 'Surely I have acted like a fool and have erred greatly.' (I must say that the older AV rendering sounds more forceful: 'Behold I have played the fool.')

One could plunge straight into the story of Saul's life, or one might mention Paul's words, 'holding on to faith and good conscience, which some have rejected and so have made shipwreck of the faith', since it appears that the root of Saul's failure lay in his denial of the voice of conscience and in his disobedience. It is not a bad idea to start with one or two signposts, before using the incidents of Saul's life to show them working out in his experience.

The first general heading which seems to characterise Saul is *The failure of an early promise*. The picture we have of him (1 Samuel 9) is that of a handsome and popular young man, but one who was also humble. He was privileged to have the friendship and guidance of the great man Samuel, together with God's anointing as king. But as the story progresses, we very quickly find Saul experiencing *The frustration of a divided personality*. Saul soon became inordinately jealous of the young David, and took him for the enemy rather that the Philistines, whom he had been anointed to fight. He compounded his folly by outright disobedience and this led to further steps on a downward path. No doubt as we go along we shall be able to highlight the lessons from each step in

Saul's life by reference to other examples, biblical and contemporary. For nothing is clearer that the fact that, despite differing circumstances, many Christians are faced with the same *kind* of temptations and challenges that Saul was.

So we reach the next stage in Saul's life, which is *The forfeiture of spiritual power*. It seems that Saul was subject to the great principle which Christ himself taught, that 'Whoever has will be given more; whoever does not have, even what he has will be taken from him' (Mark 4:25). In Saul we undoubtedly wrestle with one of the perennial problems of spiritual experience; namely, how we can lose spiritual privileges, once they have been received. 1 Samuel 10:9 tells us that Saul was given 'another heart' and later on we read that 'the Spirit of the Lord had departed from Saul' (1 Samuel 16:14). (We may feel that this is too large a problem to tackle in a sermon that covers the whole of Saul's life, and it might be better to consider this particular problem in a separate message. Preaching a biographical sermon does not mean that we have to cover everything in a person's life.) Whatever the reason, Saul's life dwindles to a shadow of its former glory, and ends in ignominious suicide on the battlefield of Mount Gilboa.

Yet, as so often in the Bible, the darkness is relieved by a shaft of light from heaven. We cannot leave the story of Saul without showing that despite the human failure, there was nevertheless *The fulfilment of the divine promise*. Through much of Saul's life is intertwined the story of David, 'the man after God's own heart'. But that is another story, and one which clamours for further treatment.

To concentrate on outlines and skeletons seems rather soul-less. A skeleton hasn't quite the attraction of a live body, with flesh, complexion and personality. So it is time to move on from matters of structure to matters of content.

4

Clothing the skeleton

Our concern in this chapter is with the *flesh* of a sermon: the substance, the material and the content which provide the flesh on the skeleton. Older books on homiletics spoke of it as the *body* of the sermon. Not inappropriately. We can all admire a strong, beautiful and well-proportioned human body, especially when it is being used in some skill. We watch the hurdler, the gymnast or the ice-skater and marvel at the control, and the co-ordination of each part of the body as it is directed to a particular movement beautifully executed. Yet we are never so much conscious of the parts as of the whole. Each part is made to serve its proper function within a whole combination of things.

A sermon ought to have the same characteristics. Not simply a multitude of words or sentences scattered like seed on the wind, but an indivisible whole, whose parts are all subject to and contributing to a complete unity of utterance.

A plan

At this point we should remind ourselves of where we are. Having our text, we have worked out our basic divisions, and produced headings which express the truth in the text. The next step is to fill out each division of the text with material, to put flesh upon the bones. How do we proceed at this point?

Surprisingly, most textbooks on homiletics give little help at this point. For example, Broadus, in a classic treatment of homiletics, gives only twelve pages out of nearly four hundred to this topic, which he calls 'The Discussion'. By comparison, he gives as much space to 'Illustrations' or to 'Clarity'. Yet undoubtedly a sermon stands or falls more on its substance than on its illustrations or its style.

First we shall suggest some broad principles, and then some more detailed suggestions about filling out the body of the sermon.

Broad principles

The apprentice can only learn by doing. No amount of theory can replace actually working the task out in practice. Phelps has some good points to make about this.

> The same principle holds good in literary working. How to do it never comes from knowing only what to do. It comes, in part, from doing. It comes from failures, awkwardness, blunders, despairs, infinitesimal beginnings of success, happy hits which are never repeated, and the slow growth of faculties which a man can never outrun in composing.

The only way to learn how to preach is to preach. Of course we can learn from reading other men's sermons, from books about preaching, from listening to good (and often bad) sermons. Ultimately, however, we shall have to work, labour and sweat over our own forge.

The worth or otherwise of what a man says springs from the worth or otherwise of his mind, heart and soul. There is really no substitute for a well-stocked mind when it comes to giving substance to a sermon. To quote Phelps again:

> Sparse thoughts invite feeble utterance, even of that which a man has to say. Thoughts must crowd thoughts, that any things may come out with force. It is the full fountain which bubbles to the surface ... Fullness of mind on a subject of thought is essential to the best utterance of thought. Solid thought is requisite. Powerful utterance must be the outflow of a well-stocked brain.

So to produce good sermons, there is no substitute for having something to say. Ralph Sockman speaks of 'the stern hortatory preaching which steadily flogs the will without feeding the mind'. To this end, we may suggest that the ingredients of a 'well-stocked mind' might include such things as

– an exposure to great literature, music, great art (more or less of each according to personal preference);

– a continuing interest in theology, not simply in the latest 'popular' book on church life, or personal religion, but a grappling with the large questions which theology tries to address;

– an interest in, and immersion in, the world of people – there should be no problem here for the pastor, though it is sad that so many pastors seem reluctant or unable to relate their sermon material to the ordinary lives of people, and to earth it in everyday concerns;

– a life of deep devotion, and continual meditation on the Bible.

It may seem insulting to some to mention these factors. Some readers may wish that I had taken them for granted, but experience suggests otherwise. I remember on one occasion being told by a clergyman who later became a bishop that since leaving college he had read little other than the Bible. How commendable the latter, but how sad the former state of affairs. This is not to say that immersion in the world of books alone is the key to a well-stocked mind. Each of the areas listed above is important. No doubt each reader will want to add an area which he feels it is dangerous to omit.

Of course, it is important to try and conserve the results of your study and reading. I have to confess to failing to do this very successfully in my early days of preaching, and I have lived to regret it ever since. Here are some suggestions.

1. A loose-leaf Bible, or a good wide margin Bible, in which you write the results of your study. My own wide-margin Bible which I began thirty years ago has masses of notes. Unfortunately, it was an Authorised Version (AV), and since I now use the NIV almost exclusively, I have to use both Bibles. That is the danger of using a Bible that is superseded. (This is not to imply that the AV has been superseded because it is inferior, but simply that when I started preaching there were not the great variety of versions that exist now.) I also use a wide-margin Greek Testament in which I can freely write and underline.

2.   A friend of mine who is a well-known preacher has a large number of loose-leaf files (A5 size) in which he inserts his study material. He has files for each book of the Bible, and simply puts the material into each one in textual order. As he studies the Bible, and reads commentaries and other books, he harvests the material into what he calls his 'memory-bank' notebooks. He finds that sometimes when preaching on a text, simply to look at the garnered material in his files will present him with more than sufficient material for his sermon.

3.   Some preachers use a card index in which they store quotations, illustrations and textual material in readiness for future use. Another friend of mine does the same and has bulging arch-lever files in which he has pasted extracts from newspapers and magazines. Not surprisingly, he is excellent at the whole business of illustrations. Since he is an evangelist, it is more important for him than for most other preachers to be up to date with relevant material that speaks to the everyday awareness of his audiences.

The key to a good filing system is a good index. Unless we are careful, we shall not be able to recall what heading we put something under, and have to hunt frantically all over the place for it. The best idea is to have a list of main topics (perhaps taken from a book of systematic theology) – such as God, Jesus Christ, the Holy Spirit, Conversion, Justification, Atonement, Church, Baptism and so on – and then to sub-divide these as necessary. For example, we shall want to have separate sections for the many facets of Jesus. Jesus Christ: his Birth, his Death, his Titles, his magnetism, his place in history, etc. But it is best to keep all these different topics together rather than scatter them, since one topic may remind us of another. (This is, of course, in addition to our files of textual material in biblical order mentioned above.)

No doubt young preachers today may want to discard a system of card indexes in favour of a computer storage system. And why not. If I were starting again, that is how I would do it.

Whatever system we use, it has to be one that fits us. Not everyone can work with such a system, and may find it cumbersome, time-consuming and self-defeating. Whatever system we work out for ourselves, we have to remember that we always want to conserve more material than we shall ever use. Conservation is important, but it is a personal thing.

In dealing with the outline and headings of a sermon in the last chapter, we advised against turning to any commentaries or other books at that stage. So let us now put the shoe on the other foot and urge the importance of using as many commentaries and other aids as we can lay our hands on. C.H. Spurgeon has some excellent things to say about the preacher's use of commentaries, with his usual verve.

> In order to be able to expound the Scriptures, and as an aid to your pulpit studies, you will need to be familiar with the commentators: a glorious army, let me tell you, whose acquaintance will be your delight and profit. Of course, you are not such wise-acres as to think or say that you can expound the Scripture without assistance from the works of divines and learned men who have laboured before you in the field of exposition. If you are of that opinion, pray remain so, for you are not worth the trouble of conversion, and like a little coterie who think with you, would resent the attempt as an insult to your infallibility.

Specific lines of development

Quite often, ideas for development will occur to us while we are working on the headings or outline for a sermon. The two are not watertight compartments, but frequently flow together in one stream.

It may be helpful to look at a specific example, and return to the passage we considered in the previous chapter, Philippians 4:6,7. The first heading was *The Anxiety which threatens our serenity*.

As we begin to ponder this, thoughts begin to flow. Regardless of order or aptness, we should capture everything on paper, writing down whatever comes to mind.

Jesus spoke much about anxiety. Using the concordance we turn to the major passages in the Gospels, and list the various areas Jesus spoke about. We then try to relate these to similar causes of anxiety which are common today. As we do so, we remember the names of some authors who have dealt with this area, and note them down (e.g. Paul Tournier, Clyde

Narramore). We may wish to turn to them now, or we may
wait until we have got more idea of what we need from them.

Now we are reminded of one or two people in the church
whom we know to have an anxious spirit. We pause to think
about the way that anxiety expresses itself. No sooner do we
think about these people in our own church than we are
reminded of society as a whole, and the way it is consumed
with anxiety. If we keep a file of quotations or clippings, we
should have little difficulty in turning up some material. I
came across this snippet, which I picked up from Halford E.
Luccock: 'Some cynic tells us, "If you don't worry, you will go
to the poor-house; if you do worry, you will go to the lunatic
asylum." '

Let's turn to how another preacher, P. Scherer, explains this
process.

> As you think your way around, in and out, the titles of
> books may occur to you, books dealing with the same or
> some kindred subject – a sentence, it may be from a novel,
> bits of poetry, incidents: get every one of them down. Then
> go and page through the books; read the scenes again, and
> the poetry, though I should use poetry sparingly. Enter
> what you have under its appropriate head on your paper.
> Consult your own book of commonplaces for illustrations
> and suggestions. Read other sermons if you remember any
> on this theme which have really stirred you . . . And almost
> as important as anything else, get all this done promptly
> enough to leave you a little time for the kind of brooding a
> man can do as he goes about other tasks. Ideas will flash
> across your inner darkness when you are least expecting
> them . . . Things really do happen if after organizing your
> material, you let it stand awhile, sleep over it perhaps – I
> mean at night – and give that mysterious self of yours
> which dwells beneath the surface of your conscious life a
> chance, kindly if it will, peevishly if it must . . . to throw
> something at you out of the cellar.

Let me pick up this last point. It is important that we give
the whole development of our thinking about a sermon time
to work. After the initial work, it is vital, or at least highly

advisable, to put what we have done on the back burner to simmer for as long as possible. Obviously, the exigencies of the regular Sunday by Sunday ministry make this difficult, but it is a good motive for making our initial sermon preparation a task for as early in the week as possible.

Nor can we discount the possibility that new ideas and illustrations will occur even during the actual preaching of a message. Our preparation will never be completed.

By this time, we shall have a mass of notes and ideas which need sorting out and forming into proper shape. This is where we will probably want to work out some sub-headings to help in our outline. We have already three or four main headings which have provided the initial framework for the sermon.

For the average Sunday sermon, two sub-headings under each main heading are probably adequate. Perhaps three, but not more. Otherwise, we shall not deal with the whole sermon adequately in the time allotted. And in any case, the main divisions and sub-divisions will become clumsy and crowded.

Once again, some examples tailored to fit the theme we have already been working with will be more helpful than prolonged explanation.

Heading: The Anxiety which threatens our security.

    a) Jesus spoke much about the anxieties common to human life.

    b) Paul had learnt that lesson well – 'nothing' is the word he uses. Have we?

In our Introduction to the sermon (more about Introductions later), we will have referred to some common anxieties, perhaps with the aid of a news item, or a quotation indicating the extent of the problem in modern society.

Having set the scene we shall move to our first main heading, and announce it clearly, possibly twice. Then we shall move quickly to Jesus' teaching, spending as little or as much time as we feel necessary to get the point across. Then we move on to Paul's situation, with the reminder that he was in prison when he wrote this letter – surely a good excuse for anxiety if ever there was one! Yet he speaks of being anxious 'about nothing'. We shall stress what a tremendous goal this is, and how unattainable – until we consider the resources that God has given us. This will lead quite naturally towards the second section of the sermon in which we consider the resources God has promised to deal with the very human problem of anxiety. And so we progress, filling out the material as we go along in our preparation.

As we have said elsewhere, we do need to keep an eye on the proportions of our sermon, so that its various sections are fairly well balanced.

It might be helpful to show a timetable of a typical sermon, to give some idea of the balance between the sections (whilst pointing out the danger of making the whole process seem too mechanical).

Introduction		3 minutes
Section 1		8 minutes
Section 2		8 minutes
Section 3		9 minutes
Conclusion		3 minutes
	Total	31 minutes

This is merely a diagrammatic picture of the way a sermon ought to be timed. As Paul Scherer says, 'Maintain between the parts, in length and in content, as reasonable a balance as you can' (Scherer, 1944, p. 177). For it is quite a common failure for a preacher to spend so much time on the first point of his sermon that the second and third are rushed or eliminated. And since the first section of the sermon is quite often concerned with sketching a problem, it would be foolish to spend as much time on the diagnosis as on the cure. We all know that it is easier! Some preachers seem to delight in preaching more about sin than about the cure, namely redemption, and the results of redemption: peace and forgiveness. Sweazey expresses this point well when he writes:

Unless he plans ahead, [the preacher] will be expansive in the early part of the sermon and will have to slight the last part, which is usually the most important. It is in the latter part that the minister gives the final truth, the solutions, and the practical guidance. Unless there is careful proportioning, a sermon on Rom. 5:20 KJV, 'Where sin abounded, grace did much more abound,' is likely to have sin abounding through three-fourths of the sermon and grace much less abounding because the time ran out.

For some readers, to think of the average sermon in terms of thirty minutes will seem generous, and not realistic for the kind of congregations they serve. Others will consider a half-hour sermon too short, thinking that a diet of forty-minute sermons (or longer!) is essential for a well-fed people. My scheme is as elastic as you wish to make it! To quote Sweazey again:

> The length of a sermon is critical. If it is too short, the preacher has squandered his chance; if it is too long, it destroys the good that might have been done because the hearers have been benumbed and prejudiced against any-thing the preacher says . . . The proper length for a sermon depends largely on the expectations [of the congregation].

On our desk by this time there will be a few sheets of paper, one covered with what looks to the casual observer like scribbles, and another with a rough outline. This will have the main headings clearly underlined. There should be a number of notes under each main heading, possibly numbered and identifiable as sub-headings. These are the raw materials of the sermon, the ingredients for the pot. They aren't the finished product.

But the time has come to put pen to paper, and to produce a draft. And once again, personal preference takes over. What are you going to take into the pulpit? A full manuscript, to be read? As great a preacher as Jonathan Edwards did just that, peering closely at the page while a boy held a light over his shoulder – hardly calculated, one would think, to produce revival. But it did!

Or should we write our manuscript out in full and then leave it behind in the study? Such a practice of preaching extempore is, I suspect, more suited to a former, more leisurely age, when the pastor did not have his head stuffed full of the thousand and one things likely to be there today.

More common is the practice of taking a set of notes into the pulpit, which bring the main points and sub-headings clearly under the eye, but give the preacher freedom to express himself as the sentences form themselves. In this way, an illustration, for example, might be suggested by one or two words in our notes which will remind us of the illustration without giving its exact wording.

We can probably express the extent of our notes by a theorem: that the extent of our notes is in inverse proportion to the fullness of our preparation. Or to put it more plainly, the fuller the preparation, the fewer notes we need. Martyn Lloyd-Jones, who was called on more than one occasion the greatest preacher of the 20th century, often took no more than a single card into the pulpit, and then produced from it a mighty utterance of some forty to fifty minutes. But in this, as in much else to do with preaching, it is usually dangerous for the less gifted to copy the habits of the great. For most of us to adopt Dr Lloyd-Jones' practice in the hope that the result would be the same would probably be to court disaster. It is doubtful whether the average preacher has the brain power, the sheer genius, or the time to devote to sermon preparation that the famous occupant of Westminster Chapel's pulpit had.

The form of manuscript or notes we take into the pulpit will not concern our listeners as long as we give the impression of freedom and a sense of speaking directly to every person in the congregation. In fact, the beginning preacher should be reassured on this point. There is no need to hide his notes away; nor should he worry if he pauses to have a good look at them, or even reads a sentence or two if he wants to be precise over a point, or wants to quote exactly. After all, the whole purpose of having notes is to guide us along a path that we already know (assuming we have done our preparation properly). There are few preachers today like the vicar who committed his entire message to memory and started his sermon by ostentatiously putting his closed notebook and Bible to one side. The sermon then became a sheer feat of memory.

As for the form of notes, it is probably unwise to use A4 sheets of paper, since they are unwieldy. Half that size is a much better idea. Some will prefer a small ring file, though if it is too small, then that too will create problems. But it does have the advantage of holding the pages together, for accidents

do happen and sheets of loose paper can be sent flying with
the sleeve of a gown.

Introductions

Pascal, the Christian philosopher, used to say that 'the last
thing a man finds out when he is writing a book is how to
begin'. And it is not until one has put one's sermon outline
and quite a bit of the content down on paper (even if only in
the form of rough notes), that one should begin to think about
the Introduction. There are sound reasons for leaving the
Introduction until you have finished the outline, and
assembled much of the material for the sermon. You will then
have a much better idea of the whole, and when you come to
actually write out your notes or manuscript, there may be
considerable modifications in the way the sermon takes shape.

Nevertheless, the Introduction is important since it will be
the first thing that the congregation hears. It may well tip the
scales in deciding whether or not they give you their full
attention, or turn off and settle down for a quiet nap.

As W.E. Sangster reminded us, some sermons don't need any
introduction. You can plunge straight into the text and the
theme. On the whole, however, I'm inclined to believe that
most sermons benefit from an Introduction. The congregation
needs a little time to be aware of the sermon topic, to adjust to
the preacher's voice, and to settle down to listen. After all,
when we meet old friends we probably shake hands first and
pass the time of day, talk about the weather and so on, before
we start talking about the things that we really want to talk
about.

Introductions should generally be fairly brief. Their main
purpose is to call attention to the theme of the message. I
personally do not think it wise to state the aim of the message
in the first few sentences. Rather use the Introduction to arrest
the interest of the hearers. One might think of the old steam
engine which takes several long puffs before it picks up speed.
Or imagine the start of some of the films you've seen. The
camera moves across a landscape of mountains and plains,
with a long road snaking from the far distance into the
foreground. Then on the horizon we see a cloud of dust.

Slowly a figure on horseback comes into view. We move closer. It may be quite some time before anyone actually speaks. But the slow start heightens expectation, and engages the audience's attention. The preacher can take a leaf out of the film-maker's book here.

An oblique start is often very effective. Having announced the text, start by saying something or giving an illustration which appears to have nothing to do with the text. People will naturally be intrigued. Then move towards the main theme, and make the connection. (Make sure, of course, that there *is* a connection.)

Generally, I try to avoid opening a sermon with the words, 'This morning I would like to talk to you about...' or something similar. This seems very uninspiring and dull. Nor should we start by giving a lecture on the authorship of the book, or the historical details and background. All these things may be important, but if they are really essential to the sermon (and are not just an excuse for showing the congregation that we have done our homework!) then they are better thrown in somewhere along the line, rather than at the very beginning.

It is generally disastrous to begin with an apology. For example, what could be worse than for the preacher to stand up and say, 'I'm sorry if this sermon appears scrappy, but I haven't had much time this week to prepare.' Even if this is true (and occasionally it is), it would be an insult to the congregation who have come expecting a word from the Lord. Much better to plunge straight in, and trust the Lord to supply the deficiencies of our preparation by his special grace.

So how should we begin? Here are some suggestions.

1.   We can start with the context or the background. This doesn't contradict what I said above about *not* starting with the background. It obviously has to be done without any semblance of being a lecture, or a Sunday School lesson. Here is an example from Paul Rees.

'Thou fool, this night thy soul shall be required of thee' Luke 12:20. Jesus is telling the story of a rich man. It is the kind of story that, up to the point in the text, would make first-rate copy for any of half a dozen 'human interest' and 'success' magazines you might name. Here is a man who is rich and getting richer. It will soon be harvest time, and the crop is greater than ever. Slip over to his fine home, says Jesus, and take a peep at him, sitting there all in a brown study. His problem is one of growing success. He has just checked the estimated yield of his vast acreage against the capacity of his barns, and he has found that the old barns are not big enough. Something must be done. Expand! That is it. Expansion is the order of the day.

Paul Rees, *Things unshakeable*, p. 81.

Now that is quite straightforward. But the preacher's imagination has come into play, so that we are caught up in the fool's thinking, and the sentence about modern magazines makes it all seem very contemporary. This is not just a dry-as-dust story from the Bible, but a story which could be just as true today as then (which the rest of the sermon goes on to say is, in fact, exactly right).

2. We can start with people's experience – our own or someone else's. Here is an example from Campbell Morgan.

In all thy ways acknowledge him, and he shall direct thy paths. Proverbs 3:6. This text has a peculiar place in my heart. It has been with me day by day for three-and-thirty years. It was on the morning when I was first leaving home for school that my father said to me his last word, 'I want to give you a text for school and for life,' and this was the text. He gave it to me without note or comment, save the note and comment of his own godly life. 'In all thy ways acknowledge him, and he shall direct thy paths.'

I have not always been obedient to the injunction. I have often forgotten him, often failed in the acknowledgement commanded, but so far as I have been obedient, I have proved the promise true. He has directed my paths.

3. Sometimes an illustration or story makes a good opening. The title of this sermon by A.S. Wood is simply 'The Easter Gospel' and it is based on Acts 10:40–43. Here is how the preacher started:

There is a curious incident recorded in the second chapter of Charles Dickens' masterpiece, *A Tale of Two Cities*. The Dover mailcoach is stopped by special messenger. There is an urgent note for one of the passengers, a Mr Jarvis Lorry. He reads it. 'Wait at Dover for Mam'selle,' it tells him.

'Jerry,' he replies to the messenger, 'say that my answer was "Recalled to life."'

Jerry is not unnaturally surprised by such a cryptic answer. He sits up in his saddle like a startled man. 'That's a blazing strange answer, too,' he exclaims. And as the coach rumbles on its way and Jerry is left in the mist and darkness, he is still intrigued. 'Recalled to life,' he mutters to himself. 'That's a blazing strange message.'

Recalled to life! That is the announcement of Easter Day, and it sounds equally incredible to the modern ear.

Further introduction is superfluous. The preacher has captured his audience and announced his theme, and he is launched into the sermon.

4. We can start with a proverb or a truth, or perhaps a memorable quotation. George Morrison, a famous preacher of a former age, often used this type of Introduction. A sermon of his entitled 'Great Faith' on the words in Matthew 15:28, 'O woman, great is thy faith', begins with the words: 'The greatness of faith can often be measured by the obstacles it overcomes.' And with those words he is but a step from introducing the main theme of his sermon about the Syro-Phoenician woman. The essence of the sermon is that there were many things against her, but she broke every obstacle, and was rewarded by Jesus with the healing of her child.

The examples that I have given are not meant to be exhaustive, but simply to point out a number of different approaches. If there is one rule governing Introductions, it is this: *Vary your approach*. Unless we are careful, we may well find ourselves slipping too often into a similar approach. This is where our friendly critic can keep an eye upon us, and warn us if we start in the same way too often.

I have to confess that sometimes I sit at my desk, with my outline prepared, waiting to write the sermon, yet hesitating to write a word because I haven't got my first sentence right.

Sometimes I get quite frantic about it. I get up and prowl around, sit down and try again. I thought I was peculiar in this, until I read these words of J. Killinger: 'Robert McCracken, who was preaching minister at Riverside Church, said that even after a quarter century in the ministry he still had to work assiduously at the introduction of his sermons, *often spending an entire morning to produce one.*'

I personally believe that it is vital to write that first sentence out. I like to get up to preach knowing exactly what my first words will be. Whatever else may be left to the spur of the moment, this sentence ought not to be.

Endings

Which is more important, the introduction or the conclusion of a sermon? If we have to choose, then we must say, surely the conclusion. Campbell Morgan says, 'The last sixty seconds are the dynamic seconds in preaching.' Even if we feel that this is over-stating the case, yet there is something worth pondering here. Many sermons lose their impact because they dribble away into the sand, rather than closing with definiteness and distinctness. An impressive opening and a fine development will often be wasted or spoilt by a weak ending.

One reason may be that the preacher himself has little idea of what to say in conclusion. Trying to think on his feet for a memorable sentence or paragraph with which to round off his message, he says first one thing and then another, grasping for the elusive sentence. He should have found it in his study, and made sure he didn't lose it on the way to church.

We may be tempted to think that if our message is successful and really 'takes off', we shall be driving home with power and passion. How unspiritual it would be to resort to a prepared ending. How much better for us to use words supplied by the inspiration of the moment. That may happen; pray that is does. But to think in this way is to fall into the old trap of dividing freedom and order, as though they cannot both be under the control of the Spirit. Remember that it was out of chaos that the Spirit brought order on the first day of creation! 'The spirits of prophets are subject to the control of prophets' (1 Corinthians 14:21). But note what Paul says next: 'For God is not a God of disorder but of peace.'

The whole point of the conclusion is to draw together the main message of the sermon, and fasten it more securely in the minds of the listeners. There should be a stronger note of challenge and exhortation. The old adage that we should 'give the people something to *do*' is worth pondering. We need to be as definite in our conclusions as possible, and not let the hearer apply the demands of the message to the person sitting next to him but not to himself. If we fail to conclude dynamically or with absolute clarity as to what we are demanding from our listeners, it is usually because we have not thought this out ourselves.

How then should we conclude? Before giving actual examples, I would like to lay down one or two principles about ending a sermon. As with so much else, we shall find experience the best teacher, and if we continue to reflect on what we are doing, then we shall be aware of some of these principles. But it is only right that we should set out these fundamentals here for the sake of clarity, and to enable us to watch out for them and to lay good foundations (hopefully) before bad habits creep up on us unawares. So then, here are some guidelines.

1.   The last sentence is particularly important.

The reader will remember that we suggested very strongly that he should write out the first sentence of his sermon, so there is no possible uncertainty about how he is to begin. At least, that's how it seems to me. I believe that the same rule applies for the last sentence. And let me call as witness Dr John Hutton, once the colleague and then the successor of the legendary Alexander Whyte. He writes:

> For extemporaneous preaching [i.e. preaching without a full manuscript] there is one rule I would give. Write out what you propose shall be your last sentence and speak that sentence as you proposed you should. Do not allow the warmth of the moment to lead you into expanding it. If you would like to say more, don't. You may take it that *the more* you would like to say, the more which has been suggested by what you have said, has suggested itself to your hearers also . . . How often has one seen a good man talking on and

on, with his eyes beginning to turn to the back of his head, searching for a suitable sentence on which to sit down.

2.   The conclusion should be the summation of everything that has gone before. The end of a sermon should not present new material, or new ideas. The time for that is gone. (Preachers sometimes give the impression that they will never get to preach again, and must say everything that there is to be said about a subject. The result is often to destroy much of the good that they have done, by overtaxing the congregation's powers of concentration and its patience. Ninety-nine times out of a hundred, there's another Sunday to come!) It is much more important to crystallise the message, and draw together the implications of that message for the people. Campbell Morgan put it like this:

> A conclusion must conclude. And in order to conclude well it must include. In order to conclude perfectly, it must preclude. When we are concluding we are concluding. We are bringing everything to an end. A conclusion must include the things that have been said, as to their spiritual and moral impact and appeal; and it must preclude the possibility that those who listen may escape from the message.

3.   The conclusion should make demands. Almost inevitably, a sermon moves to a climax (or better, a series of climaxes). Unlike a lecture, which is simply the explanation of a topic, a sermon aims to produce change. (The definition of preaching which we adopted in chapter one stressed this element when it spoke of 'eliciting behavioural change'.) It doesn't matter whether we think in terms of persuasion, commitment, conversion or some other change, the preacher wants something to happen in the lives of his hearers. He wants a similar response to the one which the crowd made to the Apostles on the Day of Pentecost: 'Brothers, what shall we do?' (Acts 2:37). This is always the result of preaching which is effective. People recognise that the Gospel is making demands upon them, and it is up to the preacher to spell out as clearly and definitely as he can what the demands of the Gospel are.

This is another way of saying that preaching has a strong ethical content.

As for what demands are made, that can only be decided by the text itself. All we can say is that the more specific we can be in defining the challenge of our message, the better. Our appeal to the unbeliever is not simply to believe the Gospel, but to respond to it by repentance and faith. Christians need to be challenged not only to live a better Christian life, but also specifically in the areas of stewardship, family life, fellowship, witnessing and so on. If we read the New Testament letters, we will discover that the demands of the Gospel are rooted in life situations, and not simply in abstract concepts. To take just two examples: Paul spends a considerable time in several of his letters talking about money, and specifically about the need for the collection for the poor in Jerusalem; and he spells out in clear detail his demands for sexual purity.

Without pursuing this topic further, we need only add one thing. Love is the supreme motive both for appeal and for response in the New Testament. Love is the inner spring which results in gratitude, faith and love in action. The preacher, therefore, should follow the same pattern in his preaching. He should speak much about the love of God, and use that as the lever by which to move the hearts of men. He should also speak much of the obligation we have to love others.

4. The best conclusions leave the hearers with a strong sense of Christ. Insofar as Christianity is Christ, to say that sermons should be full of Christ is to state the obvious. Yet we need to be reminded of the obvious, since we do tend to forget it sometimes. For example, our preaching on the Old Testament should finish with Christ, even if he is not central. As blood flows to every part of the body from the heart, and to the heart from every part of the body, so every sermon should proceed from Christ, and flow to him.

Sometimes, our focus may be on our hearers and their character, their needs, their sins and their shortcomings. Sometimes the focus will be on our church, or on our nation and the world. But in the end, we shall not satisfy either our people or the Lord if we do not come back to him, pointing to him as the answer to every need, the Saviour from every sin, and the hope of church and nation.

A. J. Gossip, in his memorable lectures on preaching, said:

> Our business is to get people to close with Christ, to live the
> Christ-like life. And certainly, as I think, in present-day
> preaching there is a sad lack of this note of appeal, of
> urgency, of agony, of the impression that it matters
> immeasurably to them and to us that things should come to
> a crisis; this eager pleading for a verdict here and now.

These are some of the principles for ending a sermon. Now
for some examples. In fact, it is much more difficult to use
short extracts of endings than beginnings. Endings depend so
much more on what has gone before, and most conclusions
when written down cannot convey such important elements as
voice, urgency, appeal. Still, we can find some value in the
following examples.

1. The sermon by Campbell Morgan was entitled 'The
darkness of Golgotha', based on Matthew 27:45.

> I do not know what happened in the darkness, but this I
> know, that as I have come to the Cross and received the
> suggestions of its material unveiling, I have found my
> heart, my spirit, my life brought into a realm of healing
> spices, to the consciousness of the forgiveness of sins. And
> there is no other way and there is no other gospel of
> forgiveness.
>
> In the darkness he saved not himself, but he saved me. He
> declined to move toward his own deliverance in order that
> he might loose me from my sin. Out of the darkness has
> come a light. The word spoken to Cyrus long ago has been
> fulfilled in the spiritual glory of the Son of God, 'I will give
> thee the treasures of darkness.'
>
> From the sixth hour until the ninth hour there was
> darkness over all the land, and from the darkness have come
> the treasures of pardon, and peace, of power, and of purity.
>
> *Westminster Pulpit*, vol. VII, p. 207.

The appeal here is not pressed home, but this may be
because in this example (and probably the others we are using)

the original has been edited for publication. What is significant is the strong sense of unity which pervades the sermon – the theme of darkness – but the thought is subtly transformed to show that the darkness was nevertheless productive of light.

2.   A good ending can be made with the verse of a hymn. Here is another example from Campbell Morgan. The theme was based on Jesus' saying in John 15:5, 'I am the true Vine; you are the branches . . . Apart from me you can do nothing.'

> 'Apart from Me ye can do nothing.' There is no vision, no passion, no mission apart from Christ. All the failure of interest and effort in regard to missionary work results from poverty of life. The things which sever, what are they? In the unity of the vine, schism. In the individual branches, selfishness and sin. What is the remedy for all missionary failure? Not demonstration, not literature, not raising of funds. What, then, is the cure? Life, more life.
>
> The vine from every *living* limb bleeds wine;
> Is it the poorer for that spirit shed?
>
> Measure thy life by loss instead of gain;
>   Not by the wine drunk, but by the wine poured out;
> For Love's strength standeth in Love's sacrifice;
>   And who suffers most hath most to give.
>
> *Westminster Pulpit*, vol. VII, p. 272.

3.   An effective conclusion can be made with an illustration. If you leave a strong image in the mind's-eye of your hearers, they will be likely to remember the main idea of the sermon, if the two are carefully linked. Here is an example from A.J. Gossip. The theme is 'What Christ means by a good man', and the final moments of the sermon underline the difficulty some may find in claiming to be able to be the kind of person that Christ finds good. The preacher concludes:

> Only, you remember Bunyan, how the evangelist asked, 'Do you see yonder wicket gate?' And the man answered, 'No, I don't.'
>   'Well, do you see that shining light?' he was next asked, and he replied, 'I think I do.'

'Keep that light in your eye, and you will reach the goal in time,' so he was told.

Let us, too, keep our eyes on Christ and follow Him on to the end of all we see to be His will, as that will becomes ever fuller to us. And in us also it will all come true at last.

The Hero in thy Soul, p. 143.

These are but samples, and doubtless unsatisfactory because divorced from the body of the sermon. They are simply given to suggest some lines of thought concerning sermon endings. Once again, let every preacher find what suits the situation best, and remain sensitive to the needs of the listeners.

One thing that is frequently fitting is to suggest a brief prayer in which the preacher and listeners pray over the area of teaching, and together commit themselves to the main thrust and demand of the text. This will give the preacher the chance to identify himself with the people to whom he has been preaching, and also to bow together under the authority of the Word of God.

Application

The final matter which we need to discuss in the area of preparation is that of application.

The whole preaching process may be expressed in terms of taking the truth of Scripture and then applying it to the lives of the hearers. That bare way of stating the case really hides a complex process. First, it assumes that the preacher will have no problem in knowing what the truth of Scripture is. In fact, as any listener to half a dozen sermons knows, preachers often seem to have a very vague idea of the truth that their chosen text is supposed to contain. Many preachers fail here, either because they have not mastered the process of hermeneutics (biblical interpretation), or because they have imposed their own interpretation, or because they have not dug deeply enough in the text to come up with the real meaning.

But even assuming that we have got hold of the truth in the text, the whole question of application is a tricky one. In what sense, for example, does an historical incident that happened to the children of Israel have a moral application to a

congregation of Americans or Englishmen today? Or the
message of Paul, which seems so straightforward at times and
so obscure at others?

These questions indicate how important it is for the
preacher to be engaged in the search for well-founded herm-
eneutic principles. No theological debate is as important to
the preacher as this. So coupled with the study of preaching, it
goes almost without saying that the preacher will want to
continue to be interested in questions of biblical interpretation.
He may do this by studying commentaries, reading theology,
and reading books and magazines which will stimulate him
intellectually.

The question of interpretation of the biblical text focuses on
one side of the issue of application. The other side concerns
the people we are preaching to. From one angle, it is certainly
true that the preacher who knows 'Man' from the scriptural
standpoint, as a creature of God, as a sinner, and as one whom
Christ came to save, is in a good position to apply the truths of
Scripture. One has only to read the sermons of the Puritans in
the 17th and 18th centuries to know that a training in modern
psychology is not absolutely necessary to an accurate and
searching understanding of men and their needs. Nevertheless,
an awareness of the life-situation of our hearers is an essential
that we neglect at our peril.

Some preachers give the impression that they are so caught
up with the universal truths of Scripture that their preaching
is never earthed in the concrete situation of their listeners. It
lacks the pastoral dimension. Yet how can the listener believe
what the preacher is saying, if he suspects that the preacher
doesn't feel a sense of identity with him? At his desk, with the
open Bible before him, the preacher ought to picture his
hearers, and try to see beyond the surface to the deeper levels of
their condition. If he is a pastor preaching regularly to the
same people week by week, that will bring a dimension of
sympathy and insight – or it ought to. He knows the secrets
of men's hearts in a way that only God knows better.

You are preaching to lay hold desperately on life, broken
life, hurt life, soiled life, staggering life, helpless life, hard,
cynical, indifferent, wilful life, to lay hold on it with both

hands in the high name of the Lord Christ and to lift it towards his dream. (Scherer.)

I know of no better description of the pastor's sympathy and awareness of people's needs than a passage describing the practice of an American Congregational pastor, Dr Albert Coe. He once wrote:

It is my custom to spend much time here in the church alone. I walk up and down the aisles. I sit in my pulpit, drinking in God's light through the rose window. I imagine the different individuals in the pews, seeking an intimate comprehension of each one's needs and praying for the power to meet the need in a sane, intelligent, inspired way. From my pulpit I go to the street that passes the church, see the people passing – bright faces, sad faces, the man out of work, the Negro feeling the tightly drawn cord of racial discrimination. There is a woman with all the lines of distress written on her face. There is a man seeking a divorce court with his heart wracked indescribably. There they go – unhappy faces, on which are written doubt and scorn and yearning and a thousand evidences of a lack of integration with life and the universe. All the faces reveal a hunger for reality. I reach out to all of them.

Quoted by Halford E. Luccock (1937), p. 150.

Here is a preacher who will never fly over the heads of his congregation. No man who has ordinary people in his vision will need to prove his cleverness, or get lost in theological abstractions. Whenever he sits down to prepare his sermons, the faces of those people will rise up before him, and he will write out of his deep compassion for their needs – needs which the Gospel can meet. He will long to share the love and grace of God, and the Life which alone can restore, renew, and reconcile.

Application, then, is simply the truth applied. It is preaching rooted in the needs of people. The sermon is not a discourse aimed *at* the audience, but rather a dialogue *with* them.

So how do we go about applying the truth, and not just stating it? Spurgeon said, 'Where the application begins, there the sermon begins.'

We might well begin by reminding ourselves of the teaching method that Jesus used. He often used questions. He used comparisons. 'Look how the wild flowers grow. They do not labour or spin . . . If that is how God clothes the grass of the field, which is here today and tomorrow is thrown onto the fire, will he not much more clothe you, O you of small faith?' (Matthew 6:28-30). That is immediate and personal application.

When Jesus stood up to preach in the synagogue at Nazareth, he did not spend time discussing the authorship of Isaiah, or explaining its background. He read the book, and then plunged straight in with his message. 'Today this scripture is fulfilled in your hearing' (Luke 4:21). His first word pulled the prophecy of Isaiah out of history and held it right in front of his hearers with inescapable impact.

Building on that foundation, we can suggest some points to ponder.

1.   Application is personal. It brings the sermon to bear upon the actual life of the hearers. It is making clear a relation between the Gospel and the people listening. It is therefore primarily in the second person, not the third. It addresses 'you'; it doesn't simply talk about 'him, her, them'. For example, after laying down the truth which is inherent in the text, we might go on to apply it in this way: 'I've known some people like that. Have you ever felt that? . . . Do you wake up in the night sometimes with the thought. . .?'

Some books on homiletics tell young preachers that they should use 'we' in preference to 'you' on the grounds that they need to include themselves in the challenge of the sermon, and not appear to be standing apart from the congregation. But this seems to me to rest on a false assumption. People know well enough if the preacher stands aloof from them. If we give the impression that we haven't applied the sermon to ourselves in the privacy of our study, we have lost the game before it has begun. On the other hand, if a man is sincere and humble, yet at the same time speaks with authority, with a spirit of 'Thus says the Lord', people will take it. Indeed, they expect it. The preacher is, after all, the spokesman of God whilst he expounds the Word of God.

2.   Application is in the present tense. It means taking the universal principles of life about which the Bible speaks and

fitting them to the lives of people now. Our starting point may well be that of the 8th century B.C. prophets, or the 1st century world of Jesus or Paul, but our ultimate stopping place is the 20th century. A great deal of hard and careful thought is often necessary to transpose the biblical message to our culture, but unless we do make the transposition, people will think our preaching irrelevant to their needs. John Stott speaks of preaching as being 'between two worlds', the world of the Bible and the world of the Church today, or the world of time and the world of eternity, the world of the flesh and the world of the spirit. The preacher is the bridge between them.

3. Application is particular. That is to say, preaching has not struck the target until the individual is forced to admit that the truth of the Gospel has something to do with *him*.

There is a sense in which biblical truth is eternal truth. If something that Moses, Isaiah, Paul or John said was true then, it is true now. A sermon's exegesis is the same regardless of when it is preached. Calvin or Wesley, Spurgeon or Stott would all agree that the plain grammatical, historical meaning of the biblical text is primary, and would probably all agree about the basic meaning of the major biblical themes. But they would differ widely in how they presented those truths from the pulpit. Calvin's 16th century Geneva, Wesley's 18th century Bristol, Spurgeon's 19th century London and Stott's 20th century London all differ tremendously. And preaching will undoubtedly reflect these differences. That is why there is only limited value in reading sermons of the past.

And not only in the historical setting, but in the audience and the circumstances there is a tremendous difference from place to place. So the application is endlessly varied – according to the audience (whether it is old, young, etc.), the contemporary situation (war, peace, poverty, affluence), the season (Christmas, Easter, Pentecost), or the occasion (wedding, funeral, baptism and so on).

The listener must not simply agree in a general way with the preacher's words; he must feel that he must do something now and he must know what is being asked of him. So do not simply exhort people to pray – say something about *how* to pray. 'It is better to make definite, searching application than to imply or hint at it,' says Faris Whitesell.

Before leaving this matter of application, let us tie it in with the more general question of our *aim* in preaching. Because besides specific application, every sermon has as its aim to move the hearts and wills of men. As Lord Macaulay once said, 'The object of oratory is not truth but persuasion.' In fact, in preaching it is both. The final test of a sermon is, What happens as a result? R.E.O. White puts it like this:

> Whenever we preach, it is not the enjoyment of the exercise, for compliments, for admiration, for gratitude, or to deliver our own souls; but for response. That is why we must address only those present – the absent cannot be persuaded to anything. That is why we must not remain in the scripture world, nor digress to world surveys, theological curiosities, academic hobbies, or any other theme about which response there and then in the service is impossible to the hearer.

Finally, we should never forget that the preacher is taking part in an activity in which the whole Church of Jesus Christ is involved. It is never a purely private matter between the preacher and the congregation. There is a sense in which the whole Church in the whole world is involved in this activity. That is what makes preaching such an exciting and at the same time daunting adventure. Preaching is one of the ways in which God is working out his purposes. How important then that by patient exegesis, lively presentation and careful application the Truth of God comes to life in our preaching. As Calvin expressed it, we must 'apply properly and adroitly the prophecies, threats, promises and all scripture according with the present necessity of the Church requires it' (Commentary on 1 Corinthians 12:28).

One further matter demands attention. Should application be reserved until the conclusion, when having laid out the principles which the text discloses, we turn to apply these principles to our listeners? Certainly, this might be argued from Paul himself. The letter to the Romans, for example, might be divided into two unequal halves, the first half consisting of chapters 1–11, in which Paul expounds the Gospel of Righteousness; the second, consisting of chapters

12–15, in which he sets forth the implications of the Gospel (with chapter 16 as an appendix). On the other hand, we might instance all the other epistles of Paul to support the idea that he mingles doctrine and application very closely as a general rule. We might also instance the practice of earlier generations of preachers, who sometimes appear to have reserved application until the final part of their discourse.

As an example let me choose at random a sermon by C.J. Vaughan preached in 1862 in Doncaster Parish Church. The sermon is on Luke 12:49, 'I am come to send fire on the earth' and was given the title 'The Gospel a fire'. The preacher spent almost two-thirds of the sermon uncovering the meaning of the text. Summarising the thought very briefly, the preacher explains that although the Gospel is a Gospel of peace, yet the coming of Christ brought division. Fire is a power, and so is the Gospel. It causes destruction as well as healing.

Then the preacher says this: 'Now therefore let us bring the matter home to our own hearts; and see what the lesson of the text is for each one of us.'

He then proceeds to apply the truth of the text and sermon in the realm of family life, and to individuals. He looks upon the town in which the church is set and suggests that as the Gospel is taken into the town so it will be a fire.

In this particular case, the withholding of extended application until the final third of the sermon works quite well. We must add that there are many other sermons in the volume where the application is made differently.

However, my own opinion is that, generally speaking, application has a place at every significant junction in a sermon. Whenever a facet of truth is shown up, it needs applying. It is idealistic to think that the congregation will readily apply each truth to themselves without guidance and pointed reminder. Knowing ourselves as we do, we are aware of the tendency to turn aside the sword of the Spirit, and to guide it to our neighbour, rather than let it smite our own conscience. The prophet Nathan's piercing challenge to King David, 'Thou art the man', came after the sinner acknowledged a general principle, but was blind to its application in his own case.

In this matter of application, as in most of the others we

have dealt with in this book, we have tried to show the student the options and suggest some guidelines. They are not meant to be hard and fast rules, since every preacher's personality is different. He will find that as he develops his own approach to preaching, the questions of application will be worked out in his preaching in his own personal way.

5

Painting the picture

A painting is made up of features like shape, form, colour and texture. The artist uses these elements in different proportions in accordance with his vision of his final product. Most of us could easily tell the difference between a painting by Van Gogh with his bright primary colours, and one by Rembrandt with his sombre, yet masterly colouring, his use of light and shade. In the same way the composer uses orchestral colour, instrumentation, musical form and harmony. This is what distinguishes Beethoven from Brahms, or Ravel from Debussy.

So I have called this chapter 'Painting the picture' because it is about ways in which we can enrich a sermon. When we have done the work of exegesis, structured our material and worked out what we want to say, there still remains the all-important task of presenting it attractively. Just as a symphony is more than notes, and a painting more than simply colours on a canvas, so a sermon is more than exegesis and exposition. The ideas have to be expressed, given colour and interest. Of course, the way we use words is extremely important, and I give a lot of attention to words in chapter 6. In this chapter I want to concentrate on ways in which the preacher puts colour and form together in his sermon. Naturally, I shall be dealing with the whole question of sermon illustrations. But sermon illustrations are only one way of enriching a sermon. To the average person, a sermon illustration is a story that the preacher uses to give point to a particular aspect of his message. And, yes, sermon illustrations which are stories are extremely important and useful. But there is far more to enriching the sermon than telling stories, as we shall see.

Let me set the reader a simple exercise. What follows is an extract from a sermon from C.H. Spurgeon, a page chosen quite at random. That is to say, I could as easily have chosen a hundred other extracts with much the same result. What I want you to do is to go carefully through the passage with a marker (perhaps several different colours would make the job easier) and to mark everything that is more than simple statement. It will help to know that the text is Matthew 11:28–30, and the title of the sermon is 'Rest, Rest'.

We have often repeated these memorable words, and they have brought us much comfort; but it is possible that we may never have looked deeply into them, so as to have seen the fulness of their meaning. The works of men will seldom bear close inspection. You shall take a needle which is highly polished, which appears to be without the slightest inequality upon its surface, and you shall put it under a microscope, and it will look like a rough bar of iron; but you shall select what you will from nature, the bark or the leaf of a tree, or the wing or the foot of an insect, and you shall discover no flaw, magnify it as much as you will, and gaze upon it as long as you please. So take the words of man. The first time you hear them they will strike you; you may hear them again and still admire their sentiment, but you shall soon weary of their repetition, and call them hackneyed and over-estimated. The words of Jesus are not so, they never lose their dew, they never become threadbare. You may ring the changes upon his words and never exhaust their music: you may consider them by day and by night, but familiarity shall not breed contempt. You shall beat them in the mortar of contemplation, with the pestle of criticism, and their perfume shall but become the more apparent. Dissect, investigate, and weigh the Master's teaching word by word, and each syllable will repay you. When loitering upon the Island of Liddo, off Venice, and listening to the sound of the city's bells, I thought the music charming as it floated across the lagoon; but when I returned to the city, and sat down in the centre of the music, in the very midst of all the bells, the sweetness changed to a horrible clash, the charming sounds were transformed into a maddening din; not the slightest melody could I detect in any one bell, while harmony in the whole company of noisemakers was out of the question. Distance had lent enchantment to the sound. The words of poets and eloquent writers may, as a whole, and heard from afar, sound charmingly enough; but how few of them bear a near and minute investigation! Their belfry rings passably, but one would soon weary of each separate bell. It is never so with the divine words of Jesus. You hear them ringing from afar, and they are sweetness itself. When as a sinner, you roamed at midnight like a traveller lost on the wilds how sweetly did they call you home! But now you have reached the house of mercy, you sit and listen to each distinct note of love's perfect peal, and wonderingly feel that even angelic harps cannot excel it.

We will, this morning, if we can conduct you into the inner chambers of our text, place its words under the microscope, and peer into the recesses of each sentence. We only wish our microscope were of a greater magnifying power, and our ability to expound the text more complete; for there are mines of instruction here.

Metropolitan Tabernacle Pulpit (1871) pp. 13-14.

Now I can understand if the reader's immediate reaction to that passage is to say 'I would never preach like that! It is far too flowery and fanciful. It is not my style at all.' Which is, of course, quite true. It is not my style either. But before dismissing it too readily, let me point out that Spurgeon was probably the greatest preacher of the 19th century. And keeping that in mind, let us try and discover some things about his style which may help us. It is one of the most basic of all preaching rules, that one should never ape the style of another preacher. 'This above all, to thine own self be true.' But that is not to say that one cannot profit from other preachers. So what can we learn from Spurgeon?

Firstly, the power of *images*. Spurgeon's preaching is full of powerful images. Most of the time, this expresses itself in figures of speech. Metaphor, simile, personification, metonymy, hyperbole are all used. (You may need to look up these words in a dictionary, or study them in an introduction to literature.) But it is obvious that Spurgeon paints pictures in words. Sometimes the picture is created with just a few words; at other times with many. The only part that we could call an illustration in the traditional sense is the description of the bells of Venice, and even then it is not a long or complicated story – just a few brush-strokes which bring the clash of bells vividly before us.

The place of images in the Bible is a large subject, and not one that we can tackle here. But it is only necessary to quote phrases from Scripture to suggest that the most telling words in the Bible are those which use imagery (or paint pictures).

I am the good Shepherd.

He brought me up out of the horrible pit, out of the miry clay, and set my feet upon a rock.

You are the light of the world.

A brand plucked from the burning.

Death, where is thy sting?

Like as a father pitieth his children, so the Lord pitieth them that fear him.

Beware of dogs.

And I John saw the holy city, new Jerusalem, coming down from God out of heaven, prepared as a bride adorned for her husband. (There are several images combined here.)

The prince of this world.

. . .And so we might go on.

Jesus himself was a teacher who used images constantly. Every parable, and many of his sayings, are pictures in words. And in this he was following the great tradition of the Old Testament prophets and poets who also used this method of teaching.

We might go further and say that the Hebrew way of thinking was essentially by way of the concrete. They used the language of material things, of everyday life to express religious ideas. An obvious example would be the use of the phrase 'the Lord's right hand' instead of the more abstract word 'power'. The Greek mind, by contrast, used more abstract ways of thinking. Greece produced the philosophers, Israel the prophets of the ancient world. This is an over-simplification, no doubt, but it has enough of truth in it to stand as a general truth.

If we examine the history of preaching, we find that many of the greatest preachers were word painters, and used pictures and illustrations in abundance. It is certainly true of Luther. It is even more true of the Puritans. We have seen that it is also very characteristic of Spurgeon.

The young preacher should take a leaf out of the Bible and these other preachers and learn to make use of picture language. We have to say that it does not come naturally to many of us. Some of us have to work very hard to keep our language from sinking into cold abstraction and dullness. For make no mistake, images lighten our speech. The language of theology, like most technical languages, is framed in abstract concepts. Because we become familiar with these concepts, we are prone to forget that it is a language quite unfamiliar to the average person; even to many of the people who attend church regularly. For this reason, then, our theological language needs lightening with pictures and images.

By the way, how many picture words and phrases and illustrations did you find in the Spurgeon passage? I think that you should have found at least 28.

Illustrations

Having looked briefly at the whole matter of word painting, we can move on to the important question of illustrations. We can start with a simple definition: *An illustration is anything which the preacher uses to throw more light upon what he is saying*.

As we have seen in the passage from Spurgeon, a fact, a proverb, or a story may be used as a illustration in this sense. But why use illustrations at all?

1. A good illustration attracts attention. When attention is flagging, a vivid word picture or a good story will make the congregation pay closer attention. And that must surely be good. However, as we go through these features of illustrations, we shall find that each positive factor may be off-set by a negative one. The danger of using an illustration to attract attention is that if our basic manner is dull, this particular ploy will only work so often. For some preachers, what is necessary is not simply to throw in an illustration here and there, but to try and use more picture language throughout. Without slavish copying, we could well take a page out of

Spurgeon's book here, and learn how to use words and images as skilfully as he did.

2. An illustration will make our meaning clear. We have already stressed the importance of clarity, and anything that clarifies our meaning is to be welcomed. As we mentioned just now, ideas which to the preacher are common – sacrifice, justification, regeneration, Millenium and so on – may be quite obscure to most of our hearers, even those who are generally well-educated. If we can use illustrations which make these great biblical ideas more meaningful and plain, we shall remove some of this obscurity. The essential idea of an illustration is that of shedding light, of drawing back a curtain to let the sunshine in.

Consider this passage taken from Dr De Witt Talmage, whose preaching electrified audiences in America in the late 19th century.

> Sin is a leprosy, sin is a paralysis, sin is a consumption, sin is pollution, sin is death. Give it a fair chance and it will swamp you, body, mind and soul for ever. In this world it only gives a faint intimation of its virulence; but after for a thousand quadrillion of years it has ransacked your soul – what then? You see a patient in the first stages of typhoid fever. The cheek is somewhat flushed, the hands somewhat hot, preceded by a slight chill. 'Why,' you say, 'typhoid fever does not seem to be much of a disease.' But wait until the patient has been six weeks under it, and all his energies have been wrung out, and he is too weak to lift his little finger, and his intellect is gone, then you see the full havoc of the disease. Now sin in this world is an ailment which is only in its very first stages; but after the grave, it is rending, blasting, all-devouring, all-consuming, eternal typhoid.
>
> T. De Witt Talmage, *Swimming for Life*, p. 10.

Notice here that there is virtually no theological argument, or even definition. Yet sin is so vividly described in its power and consequences, that no one could fail to realise its meaning in human life. The passage is full of images, and in particular, the image of sin as disease. (Again, let me stress that I am not advocating that we preach in exactly this way, but that we learn what we can from the example of others.)

3. Illustrations can make a difficult subject easier to understand.

Once again, I am going to begin with an example. We all know how difficult it is to explain the idea of Atonement, while recognising that it is the very essence of our faith. Here is another passage from De Witt Talmage. His sermon is about 'Old wells dug out' and is based on Genesis 26:18. He says:

> You have noticed, my Christian friends, that many of the old Gospel wells that our fathers dug have been filled up by modern Philistines. . .
>
> Bring your shovel and pickaxe and crow-bar and the first well we will open is the glorious well of *the atonement*. It is nearly filled up with the chips and debris of old philosophies that were worn out in the time of Confucius and Zeno, but which smart men in our day unwrap from their mummy-bandages, and try to make us believe are original with themselves. I plunge the shovel to the very bottom of the well, and I find the clear water starting. Glorious well of the atonement! Perhaps there are people here who do not know what atonement means, it is so long since you have heard the definition. The word itself if you give it a peculiar pronunciation, will show you the meaning – *at-one-ment*. Man is a sinner, and deserves to die. Jesus comes in and bears his punishment and weeps his griefs. I was lost once but now I am found. I deserved to die but Jesus took the lances into his own heart until his face grew pale and his chin dropped upon his chest, and he had strength only to say, 'It is finished!' The boat swung round into the trough of the sea, and would have been swamped, but Jesus took hold of the oar. I was set in the battle, and must have been cut to pieces had not, at night-fall, he who rideth on the white horse come into the fray ... Expiation! expiation! The law tried me for high treason against God and found me guilty. The angels of God were the jurors empanelled in the case, and they found me guilty. I was asked to say what I had to say why sentence of eternal death should not be pronounced upon me, and I had nothing to say. I stood on the scaffold of God's justice; the black cap of eternal death

was about to be drawn over my eyes, when from the hill of
Calvary One came. He dashed through the ranks of earth
and heaven and hell. He rode swiftly. His garments were
dyed with his blood, his face was bleeding, his feet were
dabbled with gore, and he cried out, 'Save that man from
going down to the pit, I am the ransom,' and he threw back
the coat from his heart, and that heart burst into a crimson
fountain, and he dropped dead at my feet; I felt his hands
and they were stiff; and I felt his feet and they were cold; and
I felt his heart and it was pulseless; and I cried, 'Dead!' . . .
Expiation! expiation!

> De Witt Talmage, *Old Wells Dug Out*, p. 9-10.

Doubtless, there is more than a touch of the melodramatic
here which to modern readers will seem exaggerated and
unpalatable. Yet it is not difficult to imagine the powerful
effect of such preaching. It is full of biblical images, and it
certainly conveys very clearly the inner meaning of Atonement
without getting tangled up in wordy theological explanations.
Whilst we may not want to preach like that, we can at least
learn something about using vivid images to make a difficult
subject easier.

4.   Illustrations help relate truth to life. I listen to many
sermons, and there is little doubt in my mind that one of the
commonest faults of preachers is that they remain theoretical
and abstract. Whilst they are theologically correct, and biblically
oriented, yet they do not seem to be earthed in the daily
concerns of the people in the congregation. As R.F. Horton
once expressed it, 'Abstract modes of thought grow upon us
too easily when we spend much time with books and in the
reverie of study . . . and, if a preacher studies diligently and
exercises himself in the company of great thinkers, he is apt to
become a philosopher and insensibly to drift away from
common life and lose touch with ordinary people' (R.F.
Horton, *The Word of God*, 1898, p. 284-5).

To rectify this problem demands descipline. We need to
turn constantly from our text, and to let our mind roam
through the congregation and the town where we live and the
nation as a whole to see where our text 'fits'. If we are pastors,
we shall find much material for sermon illustration as we visit

from house to house, and listen to people's need and concerns.
(Not that we should never divulge pastoral confidences; that
would be unforgivable.) We shall say more of this presently
when we come to deal with the source of illustrations.

5. Illustrations help to give variety to our preaching. I
have often said to colleagues who are evangelists, 'You
evangelists only have one sermon. 1. The fact of sin. 2. Jesus
Christ saves. 3. You need to repent.' And though I say it with
tongue in cheek, there is an element of truth in it. The skill of
the evangelist is to present that basic message in a thousand
different ways.

Billy Graham has been preaching that sermon for several
decades, yet with the same remarkable results today as thirty
years ago. What is his secret? His illustrations and his
application to his hearers are always up-to-date and fresh. His
audiences always find it easy to identify with what he
preaches, because he touches them at the point of their
everyday world. He relates to the simplest listener and to the
most sophisticated because he lives in the real world, and gives
the impression that he is intimately acquainted with their
world, their heart, their anxieties and fears. And every preacher
can take a leaf out of Billy Graham's book. The great themes
of Scripture and the ultimate concerns of life are relatively
few – life and death, sin and salvation, our place in the
universe and the meaning of life, pain and sorrow. The
preacher will return again and again to these topics. Yet he
will vary his approach to them, just as the Bible treats them in
a multitude of settings. Varied illustrations will greatly
facilitate our task and bring a note of freshness to our
preaching.

Sources of sermon illustrations

When Shakespeare spoke of finding 'sermons in stones', he
gave preachers a clue to where to find sermon material. The
answer is – *anywhere*. Anything and everything may at some
time be grist to the preacher's mill. Donald Grey Barnhouse,
himself a master of the art of illustration, used to say that since
God created the world, everything in it has spiritual significance. Therefore everything in the world could be used as an

illustration of a spiritual truth. Once, when challenged about this, he proved it in the following way. Let him tell the story.

> I meditated on the fact that we were chosen in Christ before the foundation of the world. Suddenly I realized that in the plan and thought of God I was older than the sun, the moon, the stars, the earth, the trees, the garden and everything else.
>
> 'Since God planned me before He planned trees and lakes and mountains, and storms and sunsets,' I said, 'everything that there is was created in order to illustrate spiritual truth. Everything. I don't care what it is – the way the echo sounds if you clap your hands, the way light gleams off metal, the way paper tears, you name it – you can find a sermon illustration in it. A sermon illustration is in the things right round you.'

Barnhouse then tells of how he was sitting in a restaurant some time later, when a friend pointed to the sugar bowl on the table and said, 'Give us an illustration about this sugar bowl.' He replied:

> 'This sugar bowl looks as though it cost at least a dollar or two. If, instead of sitting in this modern, good class restaurant, we were in a cheap restaurant over on the avenue, the sugar would be in a rough, ten-cent mug. This one cost a dollar. If we went to the Waldorf, we'd probably find fine bone china. Whether you get a crockery mug, or an ordinary one like this, or a very fine one in the Waldorf, depends upon how long it has been put in the fire. The Bible says that we are vessels of honour, fit for the Master's use. You must be purged and burned in the fire to take on the proper work. Whether you are going to be an ornament cheap and dirty, or whether you will be a vessel fit for the Master's use depends on how you yield to the Lord for His work in your life.'

I believe that illustrative skill in a preacher, like the ability to preach itself, is to some extent a gift. But all the natural gifts of personality, and especially creative ones like music, art and writing, need cultivating by hard work and discipline. There are men of genius who seem to be able to use images and illustrations in preaching with very little effort. Spurgeon was one; Talmage was another. For lesser mortals like ourselves, illustrations need gathering, storing and choosing. They don't flow as from a spring; they need drawing from a well. So it is helpful, I believe, to spend some time considering the sources where illustrations may be found.

1. The Bible. The Bible itself is the preacher's commonplace book, in which he will find the most abundant harvest field for illustrating sermons. Every page teems with images and figures of speech. Look at its parables, its proverbs, its word-pictures. Before we ever start to look outside Scripture for illustrations, we should think of those which can be supplied from Scripture itself. Think for example of the Titles of Christ – Messiah, Lamb, Morning Star, Bridegroom, The Door, The True Vine, Bread of Life – and reflect how each illustrates a different aspect of his glory. Or take the images of the Church, which is likened in the New Testament to a Body, a Bride, a Family, a New Israel, or an army (to name but some).

For larger illustrations, we might recall the history, the biographies, the battles, the mountains, the parables, the miracles and the daily life portrayed in the Bible. In preaching about temptation, for example, we think of Jesus' own temptation, the temptation of Joseph in Potiphar's house, the temptation of Samson, the temptation of Elijah, and so on. The prophets are full of fascinating pictures which we can use, such as Jeremiah's visit to the potter, Ezekiel's valley of dry bones, Zechariah's horses among the myrtle trees, Isaiah's vision in the Temple and Daniel in the lions' den.

One might readily think of the way in which the writers of the New Testament use the Old: Paul using the story of Hagar and Ishmael, or the story of the golden Calf, or John in Revelation drawing upon the images of the Old Testament. Supremely, one looks at the teaching of our Lord to see a pattern of drawing upon Old Testament examples to enforce spiritual lessons. All this reinforces the principle that the expositor compares scripture with scripture to mutually illuminate biblical truths.

2. Books. Books are a preacher's tools. Just as a carpenter has his chisels, saws and planes, and the mechanic his wrenches, gauges and drills, so the preacher has his comment- aries, his lexicons and other versions of the Bible. Much of his daily labour is spent in studying the Bible, preparing Bible studies, sermons or other writing. Not only so, but he will also be reading theology, Church history, biography and, if he is wise, fiction, poetry and history. And from this reading he will inevitably find material for illustrations. How he garners and stores this material is not our present concern. But in the process his mind will absorb and lay down a store of material for the future, to be drawn upon at the appropriate time.

The field is so vast that is difficult to be specific. But one might suggest to the young preacher that he read and master *The Pilgrim's Progress* by John Bunyan, for he will find it a mine of illustrations. From fiction, my personal choice would be Dickens, that master of human life in its infinite variety, his humour, his love of the grotesque, and his deep insights into human nature. Others might be more likely to mention C.S. Lewis' *Narnia* stories, starting with *The Lion, the Witch and the Wardrobe*, or the novels by George Macdonald. Shakespeare demands attention, but the choice of poetry is a highly individual thing, and every man must make his own dis- coveries. I personally think that the preacher should never quote large doses of poetry from the pulpit, but a line or two can be effective.

Nor should we forget the hymn-book. The verse of a hymn can often press home a point, and arouse a memory in our listeners which will prove a very powerful lever.

3. News. I was going to write 'newspaper', but nowadays most of us take our news reports from television. It was Karl Barth, the theologian, who used to say that the preacher should have the Bible in one hand and the newspaper in the other. Whilst the preacher is rightly concerned to preach in such a way as to *transcend* today's news, he should nevertheless realise that for most people today's news tends to be uppermost in their minds. It is against the background of the daily record of events that we preach. There always seems to me to be something wrong with the preacher who pointedly ignores major news stories lest he be thought to be grabbing attention

in the wrong way.

There cannot have been many preachers in America on the Sunday following President Kennedy's assassination who were not compelled to make that a focal point of their sermon. And if we follow in the steps of the prophets of Israel, can we stand aside from the issues of the day? This is not to say that we should spend hours culling the latest scandal or juicy titbit from the tabloids. I was told as a young minister (was it P.T. Forsyth who said it?) that I should never read the daily newspaper before lunch, and that I should never take longer to read the newspaper than I had taken to read the Bible. These days, a preacher can keep abreast of the major news stories without even having a daily paper. When I started in the ministry, I did not take one, but found that it was more worthwhile to read a weekly magazine (such as *The Listener, The Spectator, The New Statesman,* or *Time*) where news was treated in perspective and after the dust had settled on the major stories of the week, as well as giving news of the world of art, literature and music. But it is not just the news, but the significance of it that the preacher is looking for, to use as illustrative material.

4. Nature. As I suggested above, God's world is created to reveal spiritual principles. Jesus himself used nature frequently to illustrate spiritual principles, as did the prophets. The Psalms, especially, are full of images of the natural world and its interaction with the world of men. The thought of the world as one of God's books is, you remember, the theme of one of John Keble's most celebrated hymns:

> There is a book, who runs may read,
> Which heavenly truth imparts;
> And all the lore its scholars need
> Pure eyes and Christian hearts.
>
> The work of God above, below,
> Within us and around,
> Are pages in that book, to show
> How God himself is found.

The seasons in all their variety, the world of insects, domestic pets, physics, chemistry, geology, the life of the sea,

the forest and the jungle are all grist to the mill. One word of
warning: make sure that your scientific illustrations are
accurate, lest there be a scientist in the congregation who will
suspect the truth of your spiritual teaching if your teaching
about science reveals your ignorance. One might be safer to
confine oneself to ordinary natural phenomena rather than
getting tangled up in scientific processes with which one is
unfamiliar.

5.   Life. Into this ragbag we may throw everything that will
not fit into any of our other categories. We can cite our own
personal experiences, stories about our family and children (as
long as they are not made the cause of embarrassment! - I
know some preachers who drag their children into almost
every sermon), incidents drawn from magazines or television,
illustrations from folk tales or fables (Aesop, for example),
missionary stories, humorous stories (if you can tell them
well), illustrations from our hobbies and interests, examples
drawn from business life, school, church - the list is endless.
In his most helpful book *The Art of Illustrating Sermons* Ian
Maclaren has this to say:

> To track down sermon illustrations . . . we need to cultivate
> the faculty of imaginative vigilance. Not much point in a
> blind man trying to catch a fox. To be successful in our
> search for word-pictures we have to train ourselves to be
> keenly observant and to meditate deeply on what we see and
> relate it to our lifework. One man will notice more in the
> course of a stroll down a single street than another will on a
> trip round the world. So we must keep our eyes wide open
> (someone has said that a preacher ought to have eyes like
> portholes), studying closely men and things, touching life
> at as many points as possible, watching people at their
> work, listening to what they say in common conversation,
> taking every chance we get of seeing anything exceptional
> or extraordinary . . . 'A man's study,' declared Henry Ward
> Beecher, 'should be everywhere - in the house, in the street,
> in the fields and in the busy haunts of men.'

In summary, then, we can say that the sources of sermon
illustrations are as numerous as the world is large - as the

sand on the seashore for number. All that we need to add are a few words of warning about the best use of illustrations.

1. Illustrations must illustrate. Although stating the obvious, this word of advice is not superfluous. If we use an illustration whose meaning is obscure, people will be thinking for the next five minutes of the sermon, 'What did he mean by that?' And if the illustration does not really 'fit' what we are trying to get across, people will say to themselves, 'What was the point of that?' whilst you are hurrying on to the next part of your message.

2. Illustrations should be simple and accurate. If the illustration is more difficult to grasp than the point it is supposed to be illustrationg, then you are wasting your breath. Some stories may strike us as very suitable, but if we do not think them out we may find ourselves getting into an awful tangle trying to put them across. If an illustration is too long, or too complex, it may topple over and both the illustration and the point it was trying to support will fall to the ground. For myself, I tend to leave scientific matters severely alone. On the other hand, because I know a lot about music, I tend to feel comfortable with illustrations drawn from it. The danger here, of course, is that others may not share our knowledge or our enthusiasm, and we may start to use technical terms, and so muddy the stream of our thought.

3. Do not use too many illustrations. I have known sermons (quite often 'evangelistic' ones) which have started with a long string of funny stories which have had nothing to do with the theme, and by the time the topic was reached, it seemed it was introduced almost as an after-thought. Such a practice smacks too much of the well-known process whereby a stand-up comic softens up the audience for the main attraction of the evening. This has never been a temptation of mine, because I am not a natural story-teller, and I need to make sure that I have enough illustrations not too many. But I can imagine that for some naturally gifted speakers, it may become a temptation. If illustrations are like windows, set in the building to let in light, then they should be in proportion to the whole. Glasshouses are places for simpletons.

4. Books of illustrations. What are we to say about published books of illustrations? Some writers on homiletics

abominate them. W. E. Sangster tells us to burn them. But such advice is surely too severe. Sangster himself was a marvellous preacher whose power of illustration was quite remarkable. But there are few men with that facility to draw upon boundless funds of images and pictures. It is interesting to compare this viewpoint with Spurgeon's. His third book of *Lectures to My Students* is called *The Art of Illustration*. It is interesting to note that he has a chapter entitled, 'Cyclopaedias of anecdotes and illustrations' in which he examines a large number of such books, and speaks of his own extensive use of them. One sentence is very revealing, since it suggests how Spurgeon used such books. He mentions a particular volume, of which he says, 'To me, it has been a great thought-breeding book. It has often started me with an illustration that I should never else have thought of: therefore I have good reason to speak well of it' (p. 72). This suggests that Spurgeon found such books of illustrations and anecdotes breeding-gounds for his own. That would seem to be a sound principle from which to work.

I would make it a rule for young preachers (and older ones too) that in using illustrations from collections they do not simply copy them, but take the central idea and express it in their own words. This will save them from the artificiality of using another person's language which may be very different from their own. In any case, to get hold of the essential idea in the illustration and then to put it in our words will make it more effective.

When I visit an art gallery, I always marvel at the great variety of ways in which different artists approach a subject: how the Italians differ from the Dutch, or the English from the French. The same is true of music. Equally great composers have approached the writing of symphonies in quite different ways. Indeed, it is precisely the way in which the composer's personality expresses itself through the common symphonic form which makes each symphony a new musical experience for the listener.

In the same way, every preacher is different. There will never be another Spurgeon, or Sangster or Billy Graham. Each of us is uniquely different, gifted with a separate personality, and developing through the experiences of life differently. If we were to write a symphony, or to paint a picture, it would be an expression of our personality. So our sermons are different, the illustrations that we use, and the language we use. What I would urge upon every preacher is the necessity of looking critically at his own efforts, of constantly questioning his ways of doing things, of examining his habits of sermon preparation, and sometimes trying to do the whole thing in a different way. For the danger that faces us all is to settle down into the comfortable and the customary. Just as every marriage needs freshening up, so do our sermons. So get some fresh colour on your palette, and paint a new picture.

Part II

Performance

6

Taking the stage

Our study of preaching began by using the analogy of the concert pianist. Like the preacher, there are two different, though related, sides to his life. The first is carried on in the privacy of his study. Absorbed in the music score, which corresponds to the preacher's sacred text, he comes to terms with it by evolving a certain interpretation. He then has to master the music, and by practice and practice, and yet more practice, is able to make it his own. There is a sense in which this is not only a physical and mental process, but also a 'spiritual' one, because the ideal performance is a re-creation of the composer's soul. He brings the score to life.

Yet the pianist is never merely a pipe, through which the music flows, unaffected by the pianist's own personality. This is evident when we speak the names of the great masters of the keyboard: Pachmann, Busoni, Schnabel, Rubinstein. Each brought to the music a unique dimension of his own, distinctive and creative in its own right.

The same is true of preaching. Every preacher brings the Truth to life through his own personality – to use the most famous definition of preaching. Phillips Brooks, himself a consummate preacher, seemed to capture in the one phrase the inner meaning of preaching in a way that has never been surpassed. Here are his words.

Preaching is the communication of truth by man to man. It has in it two essential elements, truth and personality. It must have both elements. It is in the different proportions in which the two are mingled that the difference between two great classes of sermons and preaching lies. It is in the defect of the one or the other element in every sermon, and every preacher falls short of the perfect standard. It is in the absence of the other element that a discourse ceases to be a sermon, and a man ceases to be a preacher altogether.

P. Brooks (1877), p.5.

These words might easily be written about a musical performance, which is why the analogy is so useful. It enables us to view our own task in a different light.

But all the labour and practice of the concert pianist would be in vain if he remained behind closed doors and never walked onto the concert platform, or into the broadcasting studio. For the whole life of the concert pianist has prepared him to be a *performer*. The years of study and preparation and the months of practice to perfect a particular programme only have significance if he is able to perform it, and to deliver his soul, as it were. The performer must communicate or perish.

The picture still holds for the preacher. We can hardly conceive of a preacher who produced a sermon every week, and then failed to stand and deliver. The whole business of preaching has to do not only with *preparation* but also with *performance*.

Preachers have proverbially been compared to actors rather than to pianists or musicians. In that the medium of communication is speech and words, the parallel is easily drawn. The well-known anecdote is worth repeating.

The famous actor Macready was asked by a preacher, 'What is the reason for the difference between us? You are appearing before crowds night after night acting out fiction with great effect; the crowds hang on your words. I am preaching eternal truth, yet I seem to be having no impact at all.'

Macready's response was this: 'The answer is quite simple. I present my fiction as if it were truth; you present your truth as though it were fiction.'

The preacher has the greatest message in the world. To say it suggests a cliché. Yet it is also true that we may have the materials of a sermonic masterpiece, prepared to the nth degree, and still fail to make of it what we ought, because we fail in the performance. Apprentice preachers, especially, so often expose their weakness in this area of performance, that we are giving an important place to this topic. Some of the

things we have to say will appear so elementary and obvious,
that some readers may think we are underestimating their
intelligence. We can only plead that our observations are
based on long experience of the kind of thing that happens
very frequently in the pulpit. More experienced preachers also,
we have found, fall into bad habits. If we do no more than
warn of the danger of bad habits and mannerisms, we shall
have done something useful.

Ian Macpherson gave this advice:

> Listen to as many sermons as you can – good, bad and
> indifferent. For, after all, if the fellow cannot show you how
> to preach, he can at any rate show you how not to preach,
> and that is always something to be gained. Sometimes you
> may have an almost overwhelming desire to leave your seat
> in the congregation and stride up to the pulpit and do it
> yourself.

Preachers don't come mass-produced. They are as diverse as
the rest of mankind. Just as soon ask 'What does a doctor look
like?' as 'What does a preacher look like?' Like most of the
professions, preachers have suffered at the hands of Hollywood
stereotypes. The popular mind tends to have an image of the
strong manly preacher type resembling Gregory Peck in *The
Keys of the Kingdom*. Equally false is the weak, bumbling
parson who is all too often the butt of humour in television
comedies.

Preachers come in all shapes and sizes, and with every
possible quirk and mannerism known to man. Some preachers
have been very impressive in the pulpit. Joseph Parker, who, it
has been said, reigned at the famous London church, The City
Temple, 'like a king on his throne', had unusual natural
endowments.

> His massive figure, and his leonine head, with its shaggy
> locks, would have attracted attention anywhere. The gleam-
> ing eyes, the sweeping gestures, the constantly changing
> inflexion of his wonderful voice, at one moment like a roar
> of thunder and the next soft as a whisper, held any audience
> spell-bound.
>
> A. Gammie, *Preachers I have Heard*, p. 40

By contrast, the same writer recalls Dr John Ker, the author of an outstanding book on the history of preaching, who was also a famous preacher in his own right. Yet he lacked physical presence.

> He was fragile physically and somewhat deformed in appearance, but when he came to some of the more telling passages in his sermons his face lighted up and transfigured with a rare beauty of its own and you beheld the triumph of the spiritual over the physical. With uplifted finger and trembling lip he would hold his hearers spellbound as, in low tones, he delivered his soft tender appeals.
>
> Gammie, *ibid.*, p. 108

No one, tradition suggests, would have found St Paul visually appealing, or much of a pulpit presence. He himself says that people said of him, 'His letters are weighty and forceful, but in his person he is unimpressive and his speaking amounts to nothing' (2 Corinthians 10:10). How we would have loved to have heard him, nevertheless.

Much the same, of course, could be said of musicians. They too appear in public. Some, like the great Paderewski, were immensely impressive when they walked onto the platform. Ashkenazy, short of stature and slight of build, has quite the opposite effect – until he begins to play. Then one is surprised that such huge power and strength can come from so small a figure.

Ultimately, as is clear from these examples, power and presence have little to do with size. For the preacher not even a powerful voice is necessary, as long as it is clear and distinct.

What is involved in what we have chosen to call the preacher's 'performance'? After the work on the text is done, the outline produced and the substance of what we have to say is decided, what then?

I would suggest that there are three broad areas which need attention and which will have a major influence on how successful the sermon turns out to be.

1. The first concerns the way we express our thoughts. This will include such things as our use of words. Words are the tools of the preacher's trade, and he needs to care for them

and be as skilled in his use of them as the carpenter cares for and uses his chisels, saws and planes. Under this heading we also ought to consider the larger topic of how the preacher creates an impression. This is more than a matter of mere words. We shall examine the two vital matters of clarity and simplicity, both of which help us to put our message across. Then we look at the preacher's enthusiasm. We might also call it by the rather old-fashioned name of earnestness, or force-fulness, or even passion. A sermon ought to have thrust, a driving force that carries it through from beginning to end.

2.   The second important area is the voice and body. The importance of the voice can hardly be over-estimated. Gestures are also significant, and whilst they can degenerate into mannerisms which irritate or detract the hearers' attention, they can also reinforce and strengthen the overall impression.

3.   The third topic concerns the man behind the sermon, the hidden life of the preacher. What goes on 'behind the scenes' profoundly affects what happens in public.

Each of these topics is important enough to merit a separate chapter.

7

Flesh on the skeleton

'In the beginning was the Word.' The preacher is not the only person whose business is words. The writer, the newspaper reporter, the TV chat show host and the advertiser all trade in words. Indeed, in their concern for the right words, and the endless pains they take to find them, they often put us preachers to shame.

Nevertheless, the preacher ought to have a reverence for words that goes beyond the verbal dexterity of much of the world's talk. After all, he speaks on behalf of the God who has revealed himself in words, in laws and commandments written and expressed in words, and supremely has communicated with man in the Word made flesh. In Jesus Christ, we have the Truth perfectly expressed. No wonder he could say, 'The words I have spoken to you are spirit and they are life' (John 7:63).

The preacher, using the divine method, is thinking God's thoughts, and trying to mediate the divine will and purpose in words. As one called by the Lord of the Church, whose will it is to express his Mind to people today, and given the privilege and opportunity to minister God's Word to a congregation, the preacher is uniquely placed. He becomes the mediator of the New Covenant.

One of the commonest pictures of the preacher in the New Testament is that of a herald. Though unknown today in the age of radio and television the herald was a very familiar figure in the ancient world. His position is defined in Grimm-Thayer's Lexicon, under *kerux*, as follows: 'A herald, a messenger, vested with public authority, who conveyed the official messages of kings, magistrates, princes, military commanders, or who gave a public summons or demand and

performed other duties.' It would be difficult to find a better
description of the preacher's task!(The most significant passage
to illustrate the parallel between a herald and a preacher is to
be found in 2 Corinthians 4:5: 'For we do not preach [lit.
herald] ourselves, but Jesus Christ as Lord.') As heralds of the
Gospel, it is our responsibility to deliver the message we have
received with authority, clarity and exactness. (See also the
chapter 'A herald' in John Stott's *The Preacher's Portrait*
[1961], pp. 29–52.)

For the moment, let us single out the *medium* of the herald's
task. He dealt with *words*. And they are of immense importance
to the preacher.

'Words are to the preacher what pigment is to the painter or
stone to the sculptor,' says Dr. Cleverly Ford, and we find the
same idea frequently in books on preaching. For though we
live in a television age, in which the place of visual images has
increased dramatically, words still retain their supreme place
in society's means of communication and, I suspect, always
will. Think, for example, of the place which chat shows
occupy on television – frequently they are boringly wordy, or
aggravating because they exhibit language badly used, or
abused. Newspapers and magazines increase in number every
week, and there is no sign of stemming the avalanche of new
books. Think, too, of family life, of industrial relations, the
place of words in Parliament and international relations.
Everywhere, in fact, words still count. Divorces follow the
breakdown in communication. Harsh words or no words at all
often lie behind the break-up of marriages or families.
Imagine the landing on the moon without the words spoken
between spaceship and mission control.

Words, then, are the most basic element in human communication (though this is not to say that other means of communication are unimportant). What every preacher needs to learn is
that *his* words are important. The preacher's words, therefore,
ought to be valued and weighed with as much care as possible.

We ought to love words

Many of the great preachers have spoken of their love of
words. This is not simply because they loved the sound of their

own voices, but because words are the preacher's tools. Alexander Whyte, prince of Scottish preachers, thought the Oxford English Dictionary (in thirteen massive volumes!) 'more interesting than any novel'. J.H. Jowett, another master preacher from earlier in this century, was sustained by 'a life-long study of words'.

This is not to say that the preacher buries himself in books, and even less that he swallows a dictionary and uses a host of long and obscure words. On the contrary, he loves words just because they enable him to express himself with clarity and exactness. He knows that in the English language (in particular) he has a marvellously flexible, rich and beautiful instrument on which to play his music. Like the carpenter who chooses the exact tool for the job, or the golfer who picks the right club to place the ball within feet of the pin, the preacher wants words at his command.

Every preacher should love the study of the Scriptures; that goes without saying. Part of that study will involve a study of the *words* of Scripture. The ability to read the Bible in the original languages of Hebrew and Greek is a huge advantage, though today this ability may be quite rare. But it is not an insuperable disadvantage if you do not have a working knowledge of the biblical languages. Many good preachers have had only an understanding of the English Bible. One clear advantage of the average preacher (and his congregation as well) is the wealth of translations available to him. Different translations of the same passage will often illuminate the meaning, and provide us with ideas which we can incorporate in our exposition. On the other hand, the Bible student needs to be aware that not all translations are the same! Different translations use different approaches to the original text, and some translations make no attempt to translate the *words* of the original but give only the *sense*. This can result in the disappearance of certain words, or at least in some confusion. For this reason, a student should not depend exclusively on one translation, no matter how highly valued it may be in the Christian community.

Consider, for example, the rich vocabulary of the Bible on 'Sin', or 'Atonement'. Simply using a concordance and tracing the use of these terms through the Bible will prove immensely rewarding, and provide plenty of material for preaching. Or ponder the many titles of Christ in the Bible. Study the various pictures of the Church used in the New Testament. Simply to explain clearly the terms that are used on these topics will feed a congregation with an excellent diet.[1]

Many other fruitful fields of study suggest themselves. For example, an understanding of figures of speech both in English and in the Bible will open doors to a deeper ability to interpret Scripture aright.[2]

We must choose words carefully

Words are like arrows – powerful when lodged in the target. Or, to change the image, 'Words, like maps, become reliable when they adequately express the experiences and evaluation they represent' (R.M. McLaughlin, *Communication in the Church*).

How important it is to ensure that the words of a sermon do the job for which they are intended. The average twenty-five-minute sermon contains about three thousand words. That's a lot of words! For this reason alone, both variety and clarity are highly necessary. Most young preachers today are probably impatient with the suggestion that they should write their sermons out in full, finding such an idea old-fashioned and tedious. But before we dismiss the idea out of hand, we should do well to listen to those who have stressed its importance. In an important recent book on preaching, John Killinger lays down as a basic principle for all preachers the following rule: You must begin by doing sustained disciplinary work on your sermons – that is, by writing them in full for a period of a year or more.

> There is no way around the sheer labour of writing. It is in the endless struggle to think deeply and write clearly that we first begin to discover what we have to say and how we can best say it.

Difficult as this advice may seem, it is advice well worth the effort. Alexander Whyte gave similar counsel. 'The reason why so many of your sermons come to nothing is that you do not write them seven times' (Barbour, 1901). Whyte's own style – lucid, exact and vigorous – stemmed from his care and discipline in using words.

Paul Scherer also lends his voice to the plea for careful writing. His words are worth noting, if only because his style of writing is a delight to read, and can only have come through giving endless pains to preparation.

> And let me say, this time with violence: I would not give a brass farthing, as a rule, for a preacher who does not write at least one sermon a week for the first ten or fifteen years of his ministry. It is a discipline that no man can afford to forego. To write only the first half and leave the second half to God as one young preacher said was his habit, merely exposes you to the compliment that was paid him: 'Sir,' remarked his monitor, 'I congratulate you, indeed! Your half is unfailingly better than God's.'

We have mentioned Whyte's love of the dictionary. Though you may not read it in quite the way he did, you will certainly want to have one within reach as you prepare. You will also need a thesaurus. The dictionary will keep you from inaccuracy, the thesaurus will keep you from poverty of expression and staleness. A thesaurus does not define words like a dictionary, but classifies ideas, and lists words in groups with the same or similar meaning. The difference can easily be seen by looking at both.

Anyone who has tried to learn a foreign language knows how easy it is to murder it by misusing its grammar or not having the right words in the right place. It takes years of effort and practice to have a good command of another language. But the preacher is not worth his salt who is not prepared to make the same effort to master his own language so that he can use it well.

'First have something to say. Then write it down as clearly as you can. That is the basis of style.' So said Matthew Arnold. And the preacher would do well to ponder those three simple sentences and apply them to his preaching.

Getting the message across

The preacher today undoubtedly has a problem in communicating with the average congregation, for most people are
largely unfamiliar with the language and imagery of the
Bible. It is hard for those who have been to Bible college and
have become familiar with the Bible as a textbook, and know
their way around the corridors of theology the way most
people know their way round their own back gardens, to
remember that most of their listeners do not share their grasp
of Bible knowledge. And it is likely that this ignorance of
Scripture will increase rather than diminish.

We should therefore assume almost nothing in terms of
what the congregation knows. The Bible contains much that
is strange and foreign to the modern reader – it is oriental,
ancient and agricultural in its viewpoint, whereas the life of
most of our listeners is Western, secular and urban. Some of
the Bible's major ideas, such as atonement, sacrifice, sin,
incarnation, sanctification, are totally foreign to modern ears.
It is useless for the preacher to bandy such terms around
without explanation and illustration. That is why John Stott
speaks of the preacher as being 'between two worlds'. He is a
bridge between the world of the Bible and the world of today,
where the man in the pew lives.

Of course, theology has its own technical vocabulary. Every
subject does. The 'shop-talk' of doctors, engineers or media
people would be a complete mystery to those who are
unfamiliar with it, because each profession has its own jargon
and language – necessary for those 'in the know'. But we
should not think much of the doctor who tried to speak to a
patient in the same terms as his medical text-book. He would
use layman's language But all too many clergymen seem to have
a tendency to use their technical language in the pulpit. They
forget that what has become familiar to them through study and
long usage is like a foreign language to their listeners. So to
speak of the preacher as an 'interpreter' is not wide of the
mark. He is like the interpreter who stands between people
who are speaking two languages and translates for them both.

An illustration from the field of Bible translation may help.
It was an awareness of the gap that existed between the
language of the old Authorised Version of the Bible and the

everyday language of some lads in his youth club which led to
J.B. Phillips' attempt to translate the New Testament epistles
(he called them 'letters') into modern English. Both he and the
publishers were totally overwhelmed by the huge response of
the public to *Letters to Young Churches*, which was the name
he gave to his translation. The response proved one thing:
people will tune in to a message that is expressed clearly and
vividly in a language that they can understand. A.J. Gossip
put it like this.

> A preacher's first task is to make himself see what he is to
> say and describe. If he cannot do that, if he cannot make a
> picture of it before his own mind, the likelihood is that he
> himself does not as yet really understand, or only muddily
> at best and is not seeing accurately and clear-cut, but
> through a fog. And his second duty is to make the
> congregation see what he sees.

Written and spoken language

This is another aspect of 'getting it across'. We should
remember that spoken language is not written language.
Spoken language uses a great deal of repetition, which would
become tedious in writing. Good writing is usually sparing in
words. But in order to get an idea across in speaking, it needs
to be said in several different ways. This is because of the
nature of speech. When I'm reading a book and I'm distracted,
or wander off in a day-dream, then I can re-read the last
paragraph or the last page. But you can't 're-read' the
preacher's words. Sermons and speeches are given in time,
which is continuous; it never stops. So repetition is natural
and necessary.

Spoken language is also less formal than written language.
To recall what we said earlier, the doctor doesn't use the
language of the medical textbook when explaining his ailment
to the patient. He has to use a different language, words that
are familiar and everyday. So too must the preacher. The secret
of J.B. Phillips' translation of Paul's letters lay here: it
exchanged the formal language of the older translation for the
common everyday speech of the 20th century, with immense
success.

Yet another factor which comes into play in speech which is absent from the written page is the way something is said, or the intonation, to use the technical word. In spoken language, we don't finish sentences; we um and ah; we smile or frown, shout or whisper. And as we have already seen, there is often a high level of repetition.

This leads us quite naturally to our next topic: clarity.

Clarity

In the course of listening to thousands of sermons by students and ministers, one thing stands out with stark nakedness: though the preacher knows what he wants to say, too often his hearers do not 'get the message'. There is a breakdown between the expression and the end result in the minds of the hearers. Not surprisingly, that is at the root of many failures in human relationships. We fail to appreciate that we are not communicating. Husbands, wives, employers, unions, and, above all, nations fail to communicate because they don't perceive what is being heard despite what is being said. For whatever reason, the meaning is not clear.

In a conversation, there is at least a possibility of misunderstanding being corrected through a continuing dialogue. Preaching, alas, can be a one-way process in which the message is distorted both through the preacher's lack of clarity and the listener's lack of understanding. I say 'can be' because the best preaching is so clear that its message and meaning are unmistakable. (Which is not the same as saying that people will agree with everything we say – they may violently disagree. But if our meaning is not clear to them they can neither agree nor disagree.) A sermon which is accurate in its exegesis of biblical truth, orthodox in its doctrinal content, correct in its homiletical form, and passionate in its delivery can still fail to accomplish much unless it is clear in its meaning to the congregation.

Clarity, then, is of immense importance to the preacher. In the nature of spoken communication, words evaporate as soon as they are uttered. They disappear instantly. There can be no going back to re-read as we can with a book. The sermon moves inexorably on – what is lost can never be picked up.

'Clarity comes from knowing the subject and from understanding it and then getting the other person to know it.' So
said Andrew Blackwood, a famous homiletics teacher at
Princeton University, who placed an immense emphasis on
clarity. His statement is outwardly so simple. But when we
begin to ponder it we begin to realise how much is implied in
those words, 'getting the other person to know it'. Too often
the preacher assumes he is making himself clear – because he
himself knows what he wants to say. Most student preachers
think they are making themselves clear. Nevertheless, a
majority fail to make themselves understood because they are
unclear in their actual presentation. In other words, what they
say is often not an accurate representation of what is in their
minds to say. There is a gap between brain and voice, between
ideas and words, and more particularly between having a
general notion of what they mean to say, and the specific way
in which it is expressed in words. Every preacher should
ponder that gap often. John Stott tells us in his book *I Believe
in Preaching* that he had a friend who was an incisive but
friendly critic and provided a response from the listener's
point of view. All preachers would benefit from such a frank
and helpful method of criticism.

C.H. Spurgeon, a popular preacher who had the ear of the
common people in a way few preachers have had, made the
point in his own inimitable way.

> Brethren, we should cultivate *a clear style*. When a man
> does not understand what he means, it is because he does
> not know himself what he means ... I believe that many
> 'deep' preachers are simply so because they are like dry wells
> with nothing whatever in them, except decaying leaves, a
> few stones and perhaps a dead cat or two.

Here are some suggestions to improve the clarity of our
preaching

1.   *Clarity of thought*. It is stating the obvious to say that
many preachers do not think enough about what they want to
say, or how they need to say it. It is hardly less obvious, but
equally important, to emphasise that very few preachers *reflect*
upon their task. After some initial training in college, most

preachers have sufficient confidence in their ability to make themselves understood and sufficient familiarity with the regular preparation of their sermons, that they cease to reflect upon their most important work. Some tend to trust in the fluency which can become second nature to them – after all, the average minister is always having to talk in public about something! Others become lazy in relation to their studies, not grappling seriously with the biblical material, losing whatever facility they may have had with Hebrew or Greek, or ceasing to tackle major commentaries. Others fail to feed their minds with a diet of good books (sacred or secular) which stretch them and demand some effort. All these factors will inevitably produce shallow thinking and thence shallow preaching. (John Stott's chapter on 'The call to study' in *I Believe in Preaching* may seem like Everest to most of us, but we need to heed the challenge to take our intellectual growth seriously.)

We live in a period of history which exalts feeling and is suspicious of intellect. A widespread scepticism about the performance and possibilities of science has led to an attitude of reliance on feelings, and an instinctive response to our problems. But an awareness of scientific method would be immensely helpful to us in our sermon preparation. Michael Faraday, the eminent inventor, once said:

> The world little knows how many of the thoughts and theories which have passed through the mind of the scientific investigator have been crushed in silence and secrecy by his own severe criticism and adverse examination; that in the most successful instances not a tenth of the suggestions, the hopes, the wishes, the preliminary conclusions have been realized.
>
> (quoted in L. Dewar, *Learning to Think*.)

Sermons may be strong in emotion, but weak in thought and substance. A constant diet of such sermons will leave the congregation under-nourished and shallow in their response to the crises of life. And people will tire of such a diet, because nothing can take the place of solid substance.

All this is relevant to the topic of clarity, since clarity emerges from hard, critical thinking, from the severe self-criticism which proceeds from careful reflection on what we are aiming at, and the way in which we are putting things across.

I believe that one aid to clarity in preaching is to have strong outlines. We should not despise the necessity of clear headings and divisions. If our thoughts are put down on paper in a logical and progressive way, they are more likely to come across to the listeners in that way too. Some preachers find the use of overhead projectors helpful in reducing their sermon material to orderly outlines. Others find the constant reference to the OHP stems the flow of their preaching too much. But having to make an outline which will fit on to an OHP transparency will often give us an indication of whether our message has a good bone-structure.

2. *Clarity of purpose, or aim*. The famous Roman orator Cicero said that the purpose of all eloquence was *action*. If we are to engage the emotions and wills of men so as to lead them to a commitment, we must be crystal clear what it is we are asking them to do. Are we seeking to instruct? To stir the heart? To quicken the conscience? To move the will? Most sermons will have elements of all these, but the total effect will evaporate unless we are clear in our minds about what we hope to produce in the lives of those who hear us.

W.H. Griffith Thomas very simply outlines three aims for preaching:

1.   Salvation: personal and present;
2.   Sanctification: full and constant;
3.   Service: hearty and devoted.

We may feel that these aims are somewhat restricted. They seem to omit preaching about current issues. We may question whether they embrace the message of the Bible in its fullness. No matter. They at least bring to our attention the importance of knowing what our sermons should accomplish. If we are dissatisfied with Thomas' list, it would be a good exercise to make a list of our own.

The idea of having a clear aim in our preaching was expressed somewhat differently by J.H. Jowett.

In all our preaching, we must preach for verdicts. We must present our case, we must seek a verdict, and we must ask for immediate execution on the verdict. We are not in the pulpit to please the fancy. We are not even there to inform the mind, or to disturb the emotions, or to sway the judgment. These are only preparations along the journey. Our ultimate object is to move the will, to get it in one way or another to increase its pace and to make it sing 'in the ways of God's commandments'.

When a preacher is in the same pulpit Sunday after Sunday, speaking to the same congregation, there is a real possibility of losing sight of this clarity of purpose. He may cease to expect change. He may be faithful in expounding the truths of Scripture without the cutting edge of an appeal for a decision. That is why it is generally easier to preach to hundreds rather than to dozens – we can safely assume that there are people there who need converting, and we are likely to respond to the challenge that they present. But the appeal to decision is not the only aim of the preacher. There is the appeal to holiness of life, the appeal to stewardship, the appeal to fellowship, to service, to prayer – the list could be expanded infinitely. Though even here, some care is needed. Some preachers become so accustomed to making an appeal at the end of every message that their hearers consciously or unconsciously say to themselves at a certain point, 'Here comes the inevitable appeal.' How boring this would be, and how deadening when the preacher really wants to stress the challenge in the text. There are occasions when no appeal of any kind is needed. Some sermons have an element of appeal which runs through-out the message.

Nevertheless, I believe that most sermons will move to a climax that makes clear the issues that the sermon has dealt with and presses home their implication for the listeners, personally and definitely.

A sermon should be like a speech concluding with a motion. This is the method of preaching. First you state your motion, and this you do when you read your text and announce your subject; then you 'speak to the motion', and this is your sermon – an exposition and commendation of the truth which you desire your hearers to accept; and finally, you 'submit your motion' in your closing appeal when you present the issue – a plain issue to be accepted or rejected.

David Smith

Simplicity

Simplicity in preaching is not the same as clarity, but it is obviously closely allied with it. They are like brother and sister.

Simplicity does not mean diluting the message. Nor does it mean making the Gospel more palatable. In our desire to get the Gospel across, we may be tempted to reduce the content of the Christian message and make it less mysterious, less supernatural. Ultimately this is self-defeating, for the Gospel will never become amenable to human reason and it can never be simplified to the extent that it is understood in purely human terms. 'I do not know who first invented the phrase. "the simple Gospel",' wrote Halford Luccock in his characteristically trenchant way. 'I hope that God, being slow to anger and plenteous in mercy, has forgiven him.'

Theology deals with the greatest truths that our minds can wrestle with, for it concerns the ultimate questions of human existence. The man who thinks that he has the truth of God wrapped up in bite-size chunks is almost certainly mistaken. The preacher, striving to communicate the Gospel in its richness and fullness, need not feel guilty if he sometimes feels that he is failing to do his job adequately, and that his attempt to make the Gospel intelligible and relevant falls short. As long as it drives him back to the task with renewed zeal to do the job better next time, rather than out of the pulpit altogether, then he is worthy of his Lord and his congregation should rise up and call him blessed. It is not easy to reach that degree of simplicity that we might desire in this world of complicated issues and intractable problems.

Having said that, the obligation rests with us to seek that simplicity in our sermons which will convey the truth to people in a way that they do understand. By every means in our power, we should break the Bread of Life small. In so doing we shall not only be following our Master, whose teaching was marked by a divine simplicity (yet which was the very opposite of shallow – it had depths that we can never plumb), we shall also be walking in the steps of some of the greatest preachers of the past.

Martin Luther said:

A preacher should have the skill to teach the unlearned simply, roundly and plainly; for teaching is of more importance then exhorting. When I preach I regard neither doctors nor magistrates, of whom I have about forty in the congregation. I have all my eyes on the servant maids and the children. If the learned men are not well pleased with what they hear, well, the door is open.

Said John Wesley:

I design plain truth for plain people. I labour to avoid all words which are not easy to be understood.

William Grimshaw, rector of Haworth, a contemporary of Wesley's whose ministry caused a remarkable revival in the north of England, used 'market language' and was reviled for doing so by the gentry. C.H. Spurgeon, whose ability to communicate the Gospel to the working-classes of Victorian London has already been commented on, urged students training for the ministry to keep their sermons at a level which ordinary folk might comprehend. 'Now as the coster-monger cannot learn the language of the college, let the collegian learn the language of the coster-monger,' he said. He was also very concerned that children should be able to understand him.

Bishop F.D. Coggan records Bishop Azariah of India as saying: 'I tell them that Jesus is alive and has come to their village and then go on to tell them who He is and what He wants to do.' Dr Coggan adds, 'That is doctrinal preaching at its simplest and best.' He goes on to remind us that the New Testament was written in the common language of the people, of the market-place and the home. This reminder about the

New Testament prompts the thought that the Gospel origin-
ally spread through the simple means of being 'gossiped' – as
it still does, to a large degree, through the witness of lay
people.

The great importance of simplicity may be driven home by
the following anecdote of the Puritan divine, Thomas Manton,
one of the supreme preachers of that great tradition.

> He was invited to preach before the Lord Mayor and
> Aldermen of the City of London, in St. Paul's [Cathedral].
> He chose some difficult subject in which he had the
> opportunity of displaying his judgment and learning, and
> was warmly thanked and invited to dine with the Lord
> Mayor. But returning to his home in the evening a poor
> man following him gently tugged him by the sleeve and
> enquired whether he was the man who had that day
> preached in St. Paul's. He replied he was. 'Sir,' said he, 'I
> came with earnest desire after the Word of God, and hopes
> of getting some good to my soul, but I was greatly
> disappointed; for I could not understand a great deal of
> what you said; you were quite above me.' The doctor
> replied, with tears in his eyes, 'Friend, if I did not give you a
> sermon, you have given me one; and by the grace of God, I
> will never play the fool to preach before the Lord Mayor in
> such a manner again.'
>
> T. Manton, *Works*, vol. I, p. xiv
> (1870 edition, with Memoir by Wm. Harris.)

In his book *Lingering in the Sanctuary*, which deals with
the Gospel of John, Adam Philip reminds us that one of the
chief attractions of that Gospel is its very simplicity.

> One of the marvels, the miracles of these chapters is the
> simplicity of their language. There is not a difficult or
> technical word in them. Of seventy-eight words in xiv. 1–4,
> sixty-four are words of one syllable, of twenty words in verse
> 20, nineteen are of one syllable.
>
> Here, no doubt, lies one secret of the words being so dear
> to high and low, to wise and simple. 'Every time I re-read
> the Bible,' Edgar Wallace would say, 'I am more and more

impressed by its simplicity. It is a simplicity that makes it the most beautiful piece of literature in the world.'

The simplicity of the Gospel of John is ultimately inexplicable. But we may suggest that it arises, in part, because the Apostle John had meditated and thought about the words and works of Jesus for many, many years. If we may believe, as most scholars do, that it is the product of his old age, then his thinking and preaching over the years had refined the elements of his experience. His memories of the days he had spent in Jesus' company stood out more clearly the further away from them he got. Old people can surprise us with the details of their childhood. It seems that memory can be refined like gold, the dross and impurities falling away to leave the residue clear and unimpeded.

How do we obtain a corresponding simplicity and transparency in our preaching? One way is to have as long as possible between the choice of a text and its final delivery in the finished sermon. Another is to preach a sermon many times – though this may not be possible for the parish minister. (There is nothing wrong, and a good deal right, with preaching a sermon many times!) One of the undoubted fruits of experience is that certain elements of the Gospel become clearer and more precious; they burrow deeper into the soul, as it were.

Forcefulness

How does it happen that some preaching puts us to sleep, and other sermons have us gripped in a vice which compels attention? The answer lies, partially at any rate, in the presence or absence of energy, power, forcefulness, enthusiasm. Call it what you like, the man in the pew recognises it when it is present, and it is an indispensable element of good preaching.

The poet Tennyson spoke of what was 'faultily faultless, icily regular, splendidly null'. If that characterises our preaching, woebetide us. There have been times in the history of the Church when enthusiasm has been frowned upon, and the hand of deadness has stilled the throb of the Church's passionate heartbeat. 'Enthusiasm' was an insult cast at the

early Nonconformists, the early Methodists, Spurgeon and the
Salvation Army. Writing of the Church in England in the 18th
century, J. Wesley Bready in his book *England Before and
After Wesley* suggested:

> Spontaneity, enthusiasm, spiritual experience were chilled
> and numbed; prayer, as the lyrical outburst of the soul to its
> Maker, was dubbed fanaticism, while cold reason was
> pronounced an all-sufficient guide of life.

It has always seemed to me that the ultimate judgement
upon our preaching of the Gospel of Christ is that people
should find it 'boring'. The most exciting Good News ever
made known to man can surely never become boring unless
the wonder of it and the light of it has become dulled to the
preacher's own soul. Of course, that is not the whole story.
Slap-dash preparation, lack of prayerfulness, a basic in-
attention to the craft of preaching, to name just a few factors,
may well have a part in producing ineffective and 'boring'
sermons. Whatever the cause, the preacher, young or old,
should take whatever steps are necessary to avoid the ultimate
insult to his preaching: tedium and lack of interest.

There is an element in preaching which goes far beyond
correct exegesis, good structure, relevant illustrations or any
other facet of good organisation. Good though these are – we
might even say, essential as these are – there is an additional
ingredient which is also essential. We may call it by a number
of names – no one word covers it entirely – but we mean that
heartbeat that makes a sermon throb with life, and moves the
hearts and minds of those who listen, indeed, which compels
them to listen. Jerry Vines uses the expression 'heart preaching'
which is as good a definition as I have come across. (See J.
Vines, *A Guide to Effective Sermon Delivery*, (1986), chap. 15.)

Campbell Morgan's trio of sermonic virtues – truth, clarity,
passion – summarise the elements of preaching well enough.
It is the passion that we have in view just now. Passion is the
quality that marks the difference between an excellent sermon
and a life-changing one.

Because this element of preaching is as difficult to discern as
the Spirit's working, seen in its effect but as invisible as the
wind, we can only attempt to describe its characteristics.

Someone wrote after listening to Dr Sangster, the out-standing Methodist preacher of this century: 'I have no difficulty in understanding where Dr Sangster's power lies. It lies in his passion, his terrible sense of urgency.' Dr Sangster's book *Power in Preaching* (1958) goes into this topic fully.

The roots of that passion and urgency lie in the preacher's love for Christ. 'Enthusiasm for Christ is the soul of preaching,' wrote James Stalker. Augustine, the greatest of the early Church Fathers, says much the same thing. 'It is more by the Christian fervour of his sermons than by any endowment of his intellect that the minister must hope to inform the understanding.'

And tracing the river back to its source, we find the very greatest example in the apostle Paul, the archetype of all Christian preachers. To study his letters is to discover a soul which felt the utmost passion for Christ and was unashamed of its feelings. 'Christ's love compels us . . . We implore you on Christ's behalf, be reconciled to God' (2 Corinthians 5:14,20). 'God has poured out his love into our hearts by the Holy Spirit' (Romans 5:5). Paul's sense of obligation lies behind all that he sought to do for Christ. 'I have an obligation to all peoples' (Romans 1:14 GNB). It drove him half-way across the world in a ceaseless urge to proclaim the Lord who had delivered him from sin and death and brought him into a glorious liberty. He was a man with a commission.

Paul would surely have approved of Campbell Morgan's words in his book *Preaching*: 'I cannot personally understand that man not being swept sometimes right out of himself by the fire and the force and the fervour of his work.'

How, then, do we get this enthusiasm, this passion?

There is no royal road to earnestness, neither can it be successfully counterfeited by an histrionic art. We can gain it only through personal conviction and pervasive love; but when we do gain it, we do not so much possess it as it possesses us and carries us out of ourselves to achievements which are as astonishing to ourselves as they are irresistible to those whom we address.

W. Taylor (1876).

He is surely right in saying that enthusiasm cannot be
worked up. We cannot write our sermons and then add
enthusiasm and passion as one adds herbs to a stew. Nor can
we portray emotion like an actor, who can convince us even
though he is playing a part. We must start further back – at
the very beginning, in fact. For our passion for Christ is
something we possess before we ever start to preach, and our
enthusiasm for the Gospel and its relevance was a major factor
in our desire to preach in the first place. So our preaching is a
result of our enthusiasm, as well as its accompaniment. The
difficulty we all experience as preachers in maintaining that
earnestness lies in the need for repeated acts of preaching.
When a preacher has to produce sermons every week, and has
to face the same congregation repeatedly, it is hard for his
preaching to catch fire. The very fact that he has repeated this
process a hundred times, that the people have heard it all
before, that the expectancy of results is low, all militate
against the glow of enthusiasm. The fire has been dampened
down by familiarity. Even John Wesley could say, 'I know
that, were I myself to preach one whole year in one place, I
should preach both myself and most of my congregation
asleep.' 'It is not the pace that kills, but the length of the race,'
said Spurgeon. Yet he reminded his students that passion,
nevertheless, had to be aroused.

> A blacksmith can do nothing when his fire is out, and in
> this respect he is a type of a minister. If all the lights in the
> outside world are quenched, the lamp which burns in the
> sanctuary ought still to remain undimmed; for that fire no
> curfew must ever be rung. We must regard the people as the
> wood and the sacrifice, well-wetted a second and a third
> time by the cares of the week, upon which, like the prophet,
> we must pray down the the fire from heaven. A dull
> minister creates a dull audience.
>
> Spurgeon *Lectures*, series 2, p. 147.

In this particular lecture, Spurgeon lists the causes of the
loss of earnestness. It may be our own physical or spiritual
health. It may be the attitude of the congregation who are
unresponsive. A small audience will also affect us, since it is

easier to preach to five hundred than to fifty. Spurgeon's remedy was the obvious one – though it is not always easy to apply to oneself. *'Our earnestness must be kindled at an immortal flame*, and I know of but one – the flame of the love of Christ, which many waters cannot quench.'

One thing is certain. This enthusiasm cannot be kindled in a moment, or put on like a suit on the morning we preach. It is the result of a habit and a character.

In one of his books Halford Luccock has a passage which sums up this subject for us. He writes:

> Emil Ludwig, discussing a few years ago the writing of biography, said that if an author is to make a subject live, he must 'live with him, think with him, eat with him'. 'Unless you have,' says Ludwig, 'a certain mad, furious, and passionate relationship to your subject, you can never make him live in the minds of others.' The task of the preacher is to make Jesus live in the minds and hearts of men. If we are to do that, we must live with him and think with him. The three adjectives which Ludwig uses are worth careful thought. They seem strange ones to use, almost weird. They are good words to hold in front of us, while we ask ourselves, would anyone imagine that we had a 'furious' relationship to Jesus? Those words of Ludwig's, by a wholly unintended coincidence, happen to be just the ones which have been used of great disciples of Jesus. 'Paul, thou art beside thyself,' cried Festus, paying a tribute to the Christ-centred life, which has been re-echoed during the centuries. Again and again observers of George Whitefield said, 'He was in a frenzy.' Zinzendorf wrote of himself, 'I have but one passion – it is He.'
>
> Mad, passionate, furious – so may it be!
>
> H. Luccock (1937), p.164.

But over against the danger of dullness and monotony, we must set the long ministries of men like Spurgeon, Simeon in Cambridge, Martyn Lloyd-Jones at Westminster Chapel, John Stott at All Souls, all of whose ministries were marked by continued freshness and earnestness. The key to such fruitfulness and energy lies in a number of directions.

Firstly, there is the inexhaustible well of Scripture. If we study the lives of the great preachers of the past (and that in itself will be rewarding and help us to maintain our enthusiasm for preaching), we discover that they had a huge enthusiasm for the Bible. Their whole energies were directed to studying and mining the Word of God in order to have treasure to lay before the people of God week by week. They exemplified the faithful teacher in the parable of Jesus: 'Wherefore every teacher of the law who has been instructed about the Kingdom of heaven is like the owner of a house who brings out of his storeroom new treasures as well as old' (Matthew 13:52). No amount of scholarship, or skill in oratory, no personal magnetism or natural gift will carry the preacher beyond a certain limited range of effectiveness. The power of preaching is the power of the Word of God, and it is only as we drink it in that we shall be satisfied with it. There are undoubtedly periods in any preacher's life when he experiences spiritual dryness, and then it will be difficult to summon up enthusiasm for the study of the Scriptures. But strangely, a faithful maintenance of Bible reading and study more than anything else will restore to him the joy of his salvation. On the other hand, there will be times when the sheer excitement of studying the Bible will make him feel like shouting from the housetops, and he will long to preach, to share what he has discovered. The truths of the Bible are the most exciting and thrilling in the whole world. We can never come to the end of the treasure-house of the Bible.

Ultimately, of course, the preacher rests upon a particular conviction about the Bible. If we are convinced that the Bible is the Word of God, it will profoundly influence our approach to preaching. It is difficult to avoid the conclusion that a loss of conviction about the inspiration of Scripture leads to a loss of conviction about its authority for preacher and congregation. We shall not necessarily look for a blinding light every time we preach. Nevertheless, we shall be continually undergirded by the belief that we always possess and preach God's Word, even if we do not have a subjective feeling that this is the word of the Lord for me today. Hopefully, on many occasions, the two things will coincide.

The second key to fruitfulness and energy is a love of

people. A preacher will never preach with enthusiasm if he does not love people, genuinely and sincerely. Now if you were to ask any preacher if he loves people, he would naturally answer, Yes. We all know that a love for people is a prerequisite for a preacher. But in fact, such a love for men and women is not so common as we might expect (and if we are honest with ourselves, we will recognise that to love people is not easy). It is very easy for us to become impatient with the generality of people, with their small-mindedness, their petty concerns, their indifference, and their slowness to respond to the claims of the Gospel. Whilst we want to reach for the stars in our preaching, most of the congregation have their eyes pretty much glued to the earth. Once again, the secret of loving people is to learn the secret from Jesus. We shall return to this topic in chapter 9.

Having spoken of the necessity of enthusiasm and passion, it is probably necessary to add a postscript to point out that this is not the same as noise or mere volume. Some preachers get very 'worked up' and throw themselves about in the pulpit. But this does not prove them to be more earnest than others who stand still. There is a kind of outward enthusiasm which can only be described as 'ranting', which the dictionary defines as 'extravagant, or bombastic speech' or 'empty declamation'. The story of the preacher who wrote in the margin of his notes 'Argument weak, shout louder' raises a smile, but shows the folly of trying to write passion into our sermons. In a word, earnestness is not the same as getting 'worked up'. Ranting probably means the end of clarity of communication, and embarrassment on the part of the congregation. No; passion is something that springs from within. It is the 'hidden fire, that trembles in the breast'. It is strong conviction, coupled with strong love, being impelled by the Holy Spirit. And that, surely, is essential for every preacher.

Endnotes
[1] There are various books which may be recommended as aids to understanding the vocabulary of the Bible. Most Bible dictionaries treat major Bible words. From a more theological viewpoint, *The New International Dictionary*

of *New Testament Theology* edited by Colin Brown (Paternoster Press) is very valuable. The *Dictionary of Evangelical Theology* edited by Walter Elwell (Marshall Pickering, 1986) is even broader in scope, and covers biblical, historical and systematic theology. *Redemption Accomplished and Applied* by John Murray (Banner of Truth) is excellent on defining the vocabulary of atonement. Two famous books, R. C. Trench on *Synonyms of the New Testament* and a similar work on *Synonyms of the Old Testament*, by R. B. Girdlestone, are still of great value.

[2] Two classic books on this topic are *The parables and metaphors of our Lord* by G. Campbell Morgan (London, 1946) and *Pictures and parables: studies in the parabolic teaching of Holy Scripture* by G. H. Lang (London, 1955). An even more famous book is Benjamin Keach's *Tropologia: a key to open Scripture types and metaphors* published in 1856. It has been reprinted by Kregel (1972) under the title *Preaching from the types and metaphors of the Bible*. It will, however, strike the average reader as far-fetched and rather antique.

8

Delivery

The pianist strides onto the platform, sits down, and appears to bow his head in prayer. Then slowly raising his hands, he places them on the keys and begins to play. As the sonata progresses, the pianist sometimes looks up and moves his body as if attempting to draw greater effort from the piano, rather like a jockey who urges his horse towards the finishing post. At other moments, his head bowed low over the keyboard, he seems to be trying to hear the quiet notes that he is stroking from the keys, although every note is perfectly audible from the furthest corner of the concert hall.

It is for this that the pianist has laboured for weeks, hour after hour. This is the moment of truth. Whatever of the music he has failed to master, and is unable to project, is now lost forever – at least as far as the audience is concerned. The feeling we get as we watch him is one of total concentration, total absorption in the music.

Some of those characteristics of great pianists prompt us to draw parallels with the act of preaching. Of course, the two things are different in many respects, yet we should be foolish if we did not gain what we can from the obvious similarities. For make no mistake, delivery is of great importance, and the various elements that make up delivery, such as voice, gestures, and mannerisms, all add to or detract from the total impact of the message. It was Alexander Whyte who wrote to a young preacher:

> Do not despise delivery, falling back upon matter. The matter is dead without delivery. Delivery! Delivery! Delivery! said Demosthenes to the aspirant. You able fellows are tempted to despise delivery as being 'popular'. I impore you

to rise above such delusion, and to do your very best by your message by delivering it in your best possible.

The reason for paying attention to delivery is simply because many speakers could improve their performance if they improved their delivery. And delivery covers more than the actual words we use and our manner of speaking. It also depends upon things like confidence, nerves, appearance as well as good voice production and projection.

Let's start with some preliminaries. For however good our material, however well-prepared we are in the study, we need to be aware of other factors which may affect the end-product.

Control

Rule Number One is to be in control of the situation. Before you get in the car to drive off to church, make sure you have your sermon notes! This may be of more than minor importance if you are preaching in a church fifty miles from home! If it is a church where you have never preached before, get to the church in plenty of time. It may help you to go into the pulpit before the service and look over the church. Is the reading desk adjustable? Is it the right height? Can you see your notes? (Some churches make little concession to things like lighting for the preacher.) If there is a microphone in the pulpit, is it working? I was in a well-known London church just the other day where the preacher went into the pulpit to preach, and found the microphone didn't work. After some minutes, by which time the preacher was trying to make the best of a bad job, a technician crawled into the pulpit behind the preacher, fiddled with the cables, and behold, there was sound! Try, if possible, to avoid such a fiasco by making sure that the sound system is in good working order – even if you are a guest preacher. Finally, when you get up to preach, are your sermon notes in order? There is nothing more disconcerting than turning over from page 2, only to discover that you are faced with page 5 of your notes. Believe me, it happens! Such attention to detail is an important factor in building confidence. Why do some speakers seem relaxed and without nerves? It is largely a matter of confidence, a highly desirable element in the speaker's armoury. Of course, this is not the same as self-confidence, or arrogance. We have not forgotten Paul's words in 1 Corinthians 2:3-4 where he says, 'I came to you in weakness and fear, and with much trembling. My message and my preaching were not with wise and persuasive words, but with a demonstration of the Spirit's power.' But Paul is not talking here about a speaker's confidence. We may be sure that Paul spoke with authority, and with great effect. Paul was greatly concerned that the Corinthians should not think that he was simply employing the rhetorical methods of the Greek orators. His power in preaching was the very opposite of oratorical skill; it depended utterly upon the Spirit of God for its effect and impact. And so must we. But it is only right that we go into the pulpit with a confidence in what we are doing, rather than uprepared and not really knowing what we are going to do.

Confidence comes from being prepared. If I go into the pulpit with a few notes hastily scribbled, and without a clear idea of how I am going to begin or end, I really ought to feel nervous and tense. I have no right to feel confident. Elisabeth Elliot writes, 'I wonder if spontaneity is not sometimes a euphemism for laziness ... Isn't it much easier not to prepare one's mind and heart, not to premeditate, simply to have things (O, vacuous word!) "unstructured"?'

But when I have mastery over my material through preparation and familiarity with it, I will not feel vulnerable and unsure of myself.

Nerves

At this point it would be good to tackle the vexed question of *nerves*. Most students who have to preach their first sermon are pretty terrified at the prospect. And it is a well-known fact that most people feel more apprehensive about standing up in public and speaking than about almost any other task they might be asked to perform.

The first thing to say is that being nervous before speaking is universal, and natural. Even the experienced preacher is liable to feel somewhat nervous when he preaches on a 'special occasion' or in a place he has never preached in before. So nervousness is not something to be ashamed of. In fact, it may be a good thing. If it is a sign that the adrenalin is flowing, that magic substance which heightens our courage and energy, and enables us to tackle things impossible, then well and good. The athlete needs adrenalin before a race, the actor needs it before a performance, and the preacher needs it before his sermon. So-called 'nerves' can be used as an ally, if they give us the impetus we need to make a good start, and convey an extra sparkle to our audience. Actually, when we are launched into our sermon, and become thoroughly absorbed in getting our message across, we forget our 'nerves'.

However, it has to be said that some people are more liable to attacks of 'nerves' than others. If you are one of these, then you will have to tackle the problem more carefully than others. You will need to be aware of ways in which nervousness appears, such as over-breathing, speaking too fast, rustling your notes, and so on. But also remember that the audience will often not be aware of your nervousness. They cannot see your knees knocking, or your hands shaking. A frozen face is more difficult to disguise, but a good rule is, *Smile*. This loosens the facial muscles and also relaxes both you and other people. And let me stress again that nervousness in young preachers often arises because they are unsure of their material, or are not sure that their message is going to 'get across'. The remedy is to do everything we can to make sure that our material is worthwhile, to pray much about our preaching, and then to have faith that God will use us.

Nervousness produces tension, and tension is a great enemy of good speaking. In fact, if we continue to experience nerves, we should examine other factors which may be influencing us without our being aware of them. Then we must look at the circumstances of our lives, and see if tensions are being produced by family life, conflict in the church, financial worries, health problems, or something else.

If problems persist, then we shall probably need to consult a speech teacher, or read some specialist literature relating to the topic.

Voice

'What do I sound like?' is fortunately easier to discover today, with the help of tape recordings and videos, than it was years ago. In the college where I teach, every student preacher is recorded on video, and the results are always a revelation to the student. Basic faults like not opening the mouth, speaking too slowly, or too quickly, standing still too woodenly, or making gestures that are meaningless are readily seen in the playback.

A good voice is a gift from God, and someone with a strong and pleasant voice should thank God for it. But many of us are not so blessed, and we should give some time and attention to making the best of the apparatus we do have.

Spurgeon had a marvellous voice, but he had good advice for those who did not. In a lecture entitled 'On the voice' (in *Lectures to my Students* vol. 1) his first piece of advice is not to think too much about the voice. He was surely right to stress that a man who has a message to proclaim, and the enthusiasm to go with it, need not worry too much about his voice. To put it another way, our first concern is to have something worthwhile to say. If we have truly worked at our material, then the message will generally get across, regardless of deficiencies in speech or manner. Nevertheless, there are few of us who could not benefit from care and attention in this area. Even Phillips Brooks, whom some consider the greatest American preacher of the 19th century, took voice lessons after he had become pastor of the famous Trinity Church in Boston – a point when most men would feel that they had arrived.

There are four basics in good speech. They are tone, diction or pronunciation, rate and volume.

1. *Tone.* 'Heresy has slain its thousands – monotony its tens of thousands,' said W.R. Maltby. There is little doubt that a monotonous voice is the hardest to listen to. We can forgive someone who murders the English language, or someone who speaks with a strong accent (such as Yorkshire, Scottish, or Cockney), but the drone of a voice which does not vary its tone will send the most willing congregation to sleep. In fact, it is impossible to speak completely on one tone, but whereas the

average speaker ranges through twenty notes of the scale, a monotonous speaker will use only five.

One of the problems of monotony (as indeed of most other faults in speaking) is that the speaker is usually unaware of it. Hence the importance of having someone who will tell us what we sound like. Monotony will not disappear automatically the more we preach. Indeed, faults in speech become deeply rooted like most bad habits, unless they are dealt with. They need specific remedies. Probably the best cure for monotony is to read passages aloud, both from the Bible and from other literature (especially drama and fiction in which strong emotion is expressed), paying particular attention to the ups and downs in the sense. One very good practice is to read stories to our children at bedtime. Using different voices for the big bad wolf and Little Red Riding Hood will encourage us in varying pitch and good pronunciation.

2. *Diction/Pronunciation.* Many preachers, when they start speaking in the pulpit, do not make sufficient allowance for the difference between private and public speech. When we are talking round the dinner table, or chatting over a cup of coffee, we can talk quietly without opening our mouths very much or taking care to pronounce our words distinctly, and we shall be heard and understood. If you watch conversation between friends, you will notice that quite often sentences are not finished, and a lot of 'filler' words are put in. Another person will cut in without having heard the first person finish, because they have caught the meaning.

But speaking in a public place, in a hall or a pulpit, brings an entirely different situation into play. Quite simply, the distance between the speaker and audience makes clear speech essential. When speaking in a church or hall, we need to make absolutely sure that we do open our mouths (even if at first it feels exaggerated to talk in this way). We have to take much more care to speak clearly. The pronunciation of vowels and consonants needs careful attention and, if necessary, exercises which help us to use them properly should be used. (A list of good books on public speaking is given in the Bibliography.)

One of the best helps in speaking one's own language properly is to learn someone else's! When we start to speak in a foreign language, how carefully we try to pronounce each word. How we have to twist our mouths to get those unfamiliar vowels right, and concentrate on getting the words out. And then how embarrassing when the native speaker looks at us blankly without comprehension. In public speaking, the same kind of care needs to be taken with pronouncing words distinctly. We should make our vowels clear, and our consonants should not be clipped, or our words swallowed.

Remember that we naturally tend to drop the voice at the end of a sentence. As I mentioned above, in conversation we don't always finish the sentence, because we have conveyed our meaning and the listener cuts in. But in preaching we can't enjoy that luxury – or laziness. If occasionally we consciously make an effort to raise the pitch of our voice at the end of a sentence, so that it finishes on an up-beat, we shall cure the fault, and it will become more natural for us to keep the ends of sentences audible.

It is equally important to stress the right words in a sentence. Let us take a simple example from Acts 8:26–40, the story of the Ethiopian eunuch.

'Do you understand what you are reading?' Philip asked.

'How can I,' he said, 'unless someone explains it to me.'

Now read these two sentences aloud, stressing the words, *you, what, are,* in the first, and *I, unless,* and *it* in the second. You can see immediately how strange and awkward it sounds. Now read it again, and find out which words ought to be stressed. Then take the whole passage, and read it through, paying attention to the words which demand stress. This is a good passage to use because it has direct speech as well as description in it. In reading direct speech (that is, the actual words someone is speaking), we must be careful not to make our ups and down too exaggerated, as that sounds equally false and stilted. Try to sound as natural as possible, remembering that because you are speaking in public everything has to be just a little larger than life.

3. *Rate.* I remember having a philosophy lecturer who spoke so slowly that he was very painful to listen to. And since he lectured after lunch, the tendency to drift off to sleep was almost overwhelming – though we sometimes wondered who was asleep, him or us! But I've also heard some preachers whose rate of talking resembled one of those incredible

American auctioneers of tobacco or cattle. We should aim for something in between.

Speaking in a church or a large hall must inevitably affect the rate of speaking. In order for our words to be heard and understood, we shall have to slow down. As someone suggested, we should let the daylight in between the words to permit the sound to carry to the corners of the building.

Speaking too quickly is often a sign of nervousness. (This is true even in ordinary conversation, as you will have noticed when someone is embarrassed about what they are saying.) Again, the remedy for the beginning preacher is to consciously slow down, making allowance for the fact that public speech needs to be slower than conversational speech.

Speaking too slowly may be a sign of depression or tiredness (and occasionally of age and the inability to produce thoughts quickly enough). Animation is a very important factor in preaching. Today, radio and TV encourage our speaking to be generally chatty and friendly, but also rather middling. Preachers should sometimes catch fire, and the preacher's enthusiasm with his message should come across strongly. When this happens, our pace picks up quite naturally, and this is as it should be. As long as we have the congregation with us, there should be no problem in making ourselves understood.

Another facet of the rate of speaking concerns the *pause*. Even in ordinary speech we pause to take breaths (even though for the most part we are unconscious of this), and we use pauses to mark punctuation – commas, full stops, even parentheses. Longer pauses will come naturally between spoken paragraphs. And in public speech these pauses between sections of the sermon can be quite long, long enough for the congregation to have a little rest before they start concentrating again.

If you have ever watched actors performing a play, you will realise just how important pauses are. 'To be, or not to be, that is the question' from Shakespeare's *Hamlet* would be ridiculous if spoken without any pauses. It generally comes across as follows: 'To be (pause), or not to be (longer pause), that is the question (longer pause still).' In the final analysis, we should learn from experience when to hurry, when to slow down, and when to pause.

Christopher Turk gives some good advice:

Silence is a more important factor in speech than most speakers realise. Silence is, for instance, the main ingredient in a comedian's timing. The audience savours the carefully judged length of the pauses before the punch line is delivered. Similarly, in informative speaking varied pauses counterpoint the meaning. Silence is a powerful way of communicating; leaving a gap leaves time for the meaning of what has just been said to sink in, and it clears the way for the importance of what is to come. But a nervous speaker unfortunately finds it difficult to leave silence. Terrified of the echoing pauses, nervous of losing the audience if he or she stops for even a moment, they rush breathlessly on, filling every nook and cranny of time with sound.

The result of continuous speaking is that the audience's minds become clogged with information. They are thinking over one fact, when the next one comes in, and then the next. There is no time to absorb, and soon the audience's minds are drowning in information. An experienced speaker, though, knows the value of silence.

C. Turk (1985), p.135.

4. *Volume*. How loud is loud? Probably we have all suffered from the preacher with the booming voice, who assaults our eardrums for the entire sermon. How relieved we are when he stops. At the other extreme, there is the voice we strain to hear, because it is as thin and soft as a dying gasp. Clearly, both are ineffective. Why play on a one-stringed instrument when we have a ten-stringed one at our disposal? The human voice is a remarkably flexible instrument, and we preachers more than most others should learn to play it well, making the most of its range and quality.

So how loud is loud? The preacher must be audible in all parts of the church or auditorium. If people are straining to hear what you are saying, they have less energy to use to concentrate on your material. Spurgeon's inimitable words are, as usual, completely appropriate:

Do not as a rule exert your voice to the utmost in ordinary preaching. Two or three earnest men, now present, are tearing themselves to pieces by needless bawling! Their

poor lungs are irritated, and their larynx inflamed by
boisterous shouting, from which they seem unable to
refrain. Now it is all very well to 'Cry aloud and spare not,'
but 'Do thyself no harm' is apostolical advice.

Macaulay says of William Pitt, 'His voice, even when it
sank to a whisper, was heard to the remotest benches of the
House of Commons' . . . It is not the loudness of your voice,
it is the force which you put into it that is effective.

As with every aspect of speaking, variety is the key to
effective communication. After all, the human voice is a
marvellous instrument with an infinite capacity for expression,
and we should learn how to use it to the best of our ability.

The body in preaching

Scientists tell us that the average sleeper turns over in bed
between twenty and forty times each night. Yet how many of
us are aware of turning over at all? Most of the time we are not
conscious of our bodies, and we don't think about our gestures
while we are talking conversationally. But when we stand up
in front of an audience, it's a different story. Most people don't
know what to do with their hands, and either stand rock still
like stone statues, or move nervously about like caged lions.
Which only goes to show that body lauguage is important for
preachers.

Some preachers have had what we may call a platform
presence. They only had to stride onto the platform, or enter
the pulpit, and immediately the congregation's attention was
engaged. We have an eye-witness account by E.H. Jeffs of the
legendary Joseph Parker, a renowned minister of the City
Temple in London, which conveys such an impression.

No other preacher has ever given his congregation such a
sense of waiting for the curtain to rise and a thrilling drama
to begin . . . When the service began the pulpit was empty.
There had been an overture on the organ, and the first
hymn had been announced by a deacon. Country cousins
began to wonder if the great man was absent and some
understudy was to appear . . . and then, as the first verse of

the hymn drew to a close, a black-robed figure, with leonine grey locks and face of rugged impressiveness, mounted slowly into the rostrum. It was the face of an actor, a prime minister, a Hebrew prophet – anything you like to imagine in the grand style: an imperious air, an imperious glance, a sort of conscious but not a heavy or pompous majesty. Great men looked like great men in those days.

The author's final sentence suggests that even when he wrote, some fifty years ago, preachers no longer had the same 'presence'. The age of great pulpit orators was already past.

We convey a great deal with the body language we use. We cannot escape the fact that preaching is an act of the whole man, not of a disembodied voice. One has only to listen to a tape recording of a sermon to realise that its impact can never be the same as the living presence of a preacher and a congregation. Whatever is created by the combined activity of the one who speaks and those who listen dies when it is over. (One can make a pretty infallible test of this by preaching in an empty church, and then preaching the same sermon in front of a congregation. Everything feels different – because everything *is* different.)

So we should pay some attention to this whole matter of the body in preaching and the kind of gestures we use. I find it most interesting that C.H. Spurgeon in his *Lectures to my Students* gives two whole lectures to the subject. They are entitled 'Posture, action, gesture, etc.' and include four pages of illustrations. Clearly, Spurgeon thought the matter extremely important. Yet though they read as entertainingly as everything in the book, they do not say anything that could not be ascribed to 'common sense'.

What we have to say will certainly not take two chapters. My view is that if the preacher thinks critically about himself, and reflects on what he is doing (especially after his early efforts at preaching), matters of gesture and body language will pretty much take care of themselves.

As we suggested previously, the living presence of the preacher is an essential element in the preaching event. I would like to add my own view that to be dressed appropriately to the occasion is important. Our dress should neither attract

attention, nor detract from the importance of what we have to
say. After all, it is the message which ultimately validates our
ministry. What we wear should, as far as possible, be a help
rather than a hindrance to the people who not only hear us but
also look at us. Within those broad guidelines, there are plenty
of options for personal taste and varying styles of dress.

Perhaps that is an argument for the preacher to wear a
preaching gown, or vestments such as are common in the
Anglican Church. A leather jacket or a sweater may be
appropriate for a youth service, but is not likely to be suitable
for a formal service where everyone else is in suits. Perhaps a
good rule of thumb is to wear what most other people are
likely to be wearing. In any case, we should be neat and tidy,
and convey the impression of being physically alert. Sometimes
a pastor's Saturday night is disturbed by a pressing pastoral
problem, a bereavement, a family crisis which has kept him up
half the night. So be it; God will give him strength to
overcome the inevitable weariness and tiredness. But there is
little excuse for tiredness on a Sunday morning if it is due to
watching TV late on Saturday night. We should make the best
impression we can as we enter the pulpit.

After first impressions, I believe the next most important
factor is eye contact. One cannot emphasise strongly enough
the importance of making eye contact with people who are
listening. It might seem superfluous to mention this at all. But
I have known far too many preachers whose eye contact was
poor. I remember more than one who had the habit of looking
in the top right-hand corner of the ceiling, then down at his
notes, and then at the left-hand corner of the ceiling. Then
back to the notes and then to the right-hand corner of the
ceiling. And so on. Only rarely did he actually look anyone in
the eye. Of course, we should not fix one poor unfortunate
listener with a beady eye and hold his gaze without moving.
Our eyes should seek out faces, and then move across the full
extent of the audience, and then move back and forward
throughout the time we are speaking. This does not mean, of
course, moving with the regularity of a metronome, but
simply that people must get the impression that we are
looking them in the eye.

There is a remarkable passage in an account of John

Wesley's preaching which confirms this point. It is by John Nelson, a rough Yorkshire stone-mason who became one of Wesley's men, the preachers under whom Methodism grew with such remarkable power. The passage is worth quoting in full because it reveals so many characteristics of great preaching.

As soon as he got upon the stand, he stroked back his hair and turned his face towards where I stood, and, I thought, fixed his eyes upon me. His countenance fixed such an awful dread upon me, before I heard him speak, that it made my heart beat like the pendulum of a clock; and when he did speak, I thought his whole discourse was aimed at me. When he had done I said, 'This man can tell the secrets of my heart; he hath not left me there; for he hath showed the remedy, even the blood of Jesus.' I thought he spoke to no one but me, and I durst not look up, for I imagined all the people were looking at me ... But before Mr. Wesley concluded his sermon he cried out, 'Let the wicked forsake his way, and the unrighteous man his thoughts; and let him return to the Lord, and He will have mercy upon him; and to our God, for He will abundantly pardon.' I said, 'If that be true, I will turn to God today.'

Quoted in W.H. Fitchett, *Wesley and his Century* (1906), p. 181.

Gestures

The preacher who is just beginning often has a problem to know what to do with his hands. This may result in his gripping the reading desk with whitened knuckles, hanging on for grim death. Or he may keep one hand in his trouser pocket and jingle his change. Or he may just keep his hands clasped behind his back. All these elementary faults stem from his hands feeling awkward, and from nervousness.

Without laying down any hard-and-fast rules about gesture (there aren't any!), here are some suggestions.

Suit your gestures to the size of the audience and the place where you are speaking. In a small hall, where the audience is quite close to the speaker, then small gestures are quite adequate. In a large church, large gestures will not appear unnatural to the congregation (though they must flow naturally out of what we are saying).

Don't lounge on the pulpit; it gives the impression of carelessness that is unsuitable for preaching the Gospel. Generally, it is bad to stand with folded arms; it rather suggests arrogance. The best speaking position is to stand upright, feet apart, with the hands free to use, or resting lightly on the desk.

Try to make your gestures fit what you are saying. Avoid holding a hand in one position, or waving it rather aimlessly a foot in front of you. Point up to heaven, open your arms to embrace the world. Sometimes rest your hands on the pulpit; sometimes keep one hand at your side.

If you wear glasses, do not keep taking them off, and putting them on. If you have a problem seeing both your audience and your notes then the only solution is to have bi-focals, or better, Variolux lenses (which are graduated from top to bottom).

Try not to blow your nose, or to drink water during your actual preaching. If you have a heavy cold, you may not be able to avoid it, but generally speaking it is an unfortunate habit. Water is also not good for the throat, and will not usually solve the problem of a dry throat.

The ultimate aim for every preacher should be to become unaware of his gestures. The preacher learns to wed body and voice together into a unity, so that bodily movements (whether of head, arms, hands or whole body) simply arise from what he is saying with is voice.

To talk about the body in preaching may strike some readers as rather superfluous. The experience of watching young preachers suggests that it is not. Many of them look distinctly awkward, and have valued at least some advice about their body movements. So we can only suggest that the reader takes from this chapter whatever advice he needs, and leaves the rest for others.

9

More than tongue can tell

We began to think about the task of preaching right at the beginning of this book by drawing some parallels between the concert pianist and the preacher. For a moment I want to return to that comparison. We noted that there are two elements which characterise them both. They both spend much time alone, preparing. But their labours only have meaning as they appear in public. We have followed them in their preparation and performance.

And now we return to their life behind the scenes. Let us make another comparison. The secret of the pianist's success is how far he manages to capture the spirit of the composer whose work he performs. In a sense, the musician must be totally dedicated to the composer. The more he is able to commit himself to the composer's mind and intention, the more time he spends in the study of the score, the better able he will be to represent the composer on stage.

And there the parallel with the preacher is very close. For the preacher has a secret life which is of absolute importance. In that secret life, he draws near to God and seeks to receive from him all that he needs to do his work. Whatever gifts he has, and whatever skills he has developed, his preaching depends ultimately upon the life he lives in fellowship with God.

There is no 'job' in all the world where the character of a man is as important as in preaching. Of course, we expect our judges, accountants, tradesmen and teachers to be people of integrity. In a sense, every profession and job depends upon the integrity and personal worth of the person doing it. Yet as we said in a previous chapter, no one worries too much if the professional pianist is not highly moral, as long as he performs well. And though we like our garage mechanic to be honest in the way he works out our bill, we are not overly concerned about what he does after he closes the workshop.

But for a preacher, it is absolutely different. His personal holiness, his integrity and his inner character are of supreme importance. If these things are lacking, then he fails. And there stands before him the judgment which Christ heaped upon hypocrites – flaming, withering condemnation. For nothing seems to have aroused Jesus' contempt and anger more than a blatant contradiction between the religious professional's word and his deed, between his heart and his mouth.

It is for that reason that so many of God's men have recoiled from the call to preach. They had a sense of innate unworthiness, which made them shrink from the task of preaching, even though they recognised the urgency and compulsion of God's call. George McLeod expressed it like this:

> The common experience of them all without exception is that not one of them wished to preach. Moses, who lived by faith, was prepared to do all that God asked of him – except to speak. Isaiah, though he saw the vision of God's glory and its relevance for the people of his day nevertheless begged to be excused from this one thing. Ezekiel pleaded that he might deliver his message in some other way. When we step outside Scripture we find a similar situation. Chrysostom shrank from the task of preaching and fought against it for many years. Augustine turned in every direction before he took the plunge. John Knox was 'pressed' by the Spirit into the ministry. F. W. Robertson begged to be excused.

Hence a book about preaching must give some attention to the question of the preacher's character. It is not a side-issue. It is central. As I write, a scandal has broken out in America over the confession by a well-known TV evangelist of his adultery. He has resigned, and the ripples have spread to every corner of the nation. The media have seized upon this scandal to berate and scoff at the whole business of TV evangelism (for it is big business – multi-million dollar business). Yet the same media look with complete indifference upon the daily torrent of adultery, dishonesty and corruption that is evident in the same TV industry and in Hollywood and Washington. Why? Because even the non-Christian world recognises that a preacher whose character denies his message does not deserve a hearing. He has lost his right to an audience.

What, then, are the ingredients which make up the preacher's secret life? I have called this chapter 'More than tongue can tell' for the very reason that it is not simply the outward man, or the words he speaks in the pulpit, that ultimately authenticate the preacher, but the hidden life. Life with God; life in Christ; life through the Spirit.

I am very conscious that not everyone who reads this book will be in full-time ministry, so I do not want to write simply for ministers. For them, there are special privileges and demands with regard to the spiritual life. For others, making time for the preparation of sermons and for the devotional life may be very difficult in the midst of many other responsibilities. Study and preparation must be crammed into crevices and corners. I suggest that for them, the secret of progress in the spiritual life is to cultivate what has been immortalised by the old monk Brother Lawrence in the phrase 'the practice of the presence of God'. How essential it is for such people to guard their times of devotion, and through the day in the midst of other duties to live in the secret place of the Most High, abiding in the shadow of the Almighty. In this way, the preparation of a message may be continued not at the desk but in the deepest recesses of heart and brain.

Let us begin to think about the devotional life of the preacher by looking at a picture.

The ideal preacher

In *The Pilgrim's Progress* by John Bunyan, Christian comes to the House of the Interpreter, and is taken into a room where a portrait is hung. The picture shows a man with 'eyes lifted up to Heaven, the best of books in his hand, the Law of Truth written upon his lips, the world behind his back'. He stood as if he pleaded with men and a crown of gold hung over his head. When asked about the portrait, Interpreter explains to Pilgrim that it is a picture of the preacher:

The man whose picture this is, is one of a thousand; he can beget children, travail in birth with children, and nurse them himself when they are born. And whereas thou seest him with his eyes lift up to Heaven, the best of books in his hand, and the Law of Truth writ on his lips, it is to shew thee that his work is to know and unfold dark things to sinners; even as also thou seest him stand as if he pleaded with men; and whereas thou seest the world as cast behind him, and that a crown hangs over his head, that is to shew thee that slighting and despising the things that are present, for the love that he hath to his master's service, he is sure in the world that comes next to have glory for his reward.

Bunyan's experience as a preacher, which included various spells in prison including one of some eleven years, show that he was no stranger to the costliness of preaching in his day. Suffering for the cause of the Gospel may not be part of our experience, although there are plenty of men and women in the world today for whom it is an inevitable result of their preaching. I remember visiting a Bible school in Ethiopia some years ago, and being forcibly struck with the fact that these men who were sitting in the classroom would very probably have to sit in prison cells in the course of their preaching careers. It was a challenging experience. There is a noble army of suffering preachers that stretches from the Apostle Paul's day to our own. Yet though we may not have that particular price to pay, in following Bunyan's preacher, there should be in every one called to preach the spiritual attitude which Bunyan characterises as 'slighting and despising the things that are present, for the love that he hath to his master's service'. For before we call anyone else to bear their cross of discipleship after Christ, we must take up our own cross and follow our Master.

This is nothing more nor less than simply to say that the preacher should be living the Christian life, and not at its lowest level but at its highest. He should be a man who has all the ingredients of Christian experience in rich abundance, and is proving his worth by showing the fruit of a godly life.

Let us examine this portrait more closely for the ingredients of the preacher's life.

The first characteristic of Bunyan's preacher is that he 'had eyes lifted up to heaven'.

It is not simply that the preacher is a man of prayer, but rather that he is totally dependent upon God for his work. Of course, prayer is an essential and vital part of this, but it is not the whole. There is a verse in the Psalms which comes to mind.

> These all look to you
>   to give them their food at the proper time.
> When you give it to them,
>   they gather it up;
> When you open your hand,
>   they are satisfied with good things.
>
> Psalm 104:27, 28.

Although the original context is of creation looking to the Creator for daily bread, it is also a picture of the spiritual life of man, who looks with faith and expectancy to his heavenly Father for the daily supply of spiritual needs. The preacher does not depend upon his own wisdom and skill in framing sermons, but must look to God for the insight, sensitivity and power that make sermons worth preaching, and worth listening to. This 'looking to God' is something in which hopefully we make progress throughout our lives. But it will never be less than a battle, and will sometimes take on the character of a real conflict in the realm of the spirit.

The preacher cannot fail to remember the example of Paul or other great preachers of the past in this matter of prayer. Too often the contemplation of the great will cast him down, rather than inspire him. Yet we dare not ignore the example of these men, nor, supremely, that of our Lord Jesus Christ. Every instance of prayer recorded in our Lord's life is instructive. Certainly, we can hardly expect to attain to his measure, but as Dean Burgon reminds us, 'The practical inference which we gather from this part of His Divine example is our own absolute need of Prayer – without which, it is feared that the most active and zealous ministrations may prove a failure; and further, that our petitions should be frequent, and earnest and submissive; and that Prayer should precede all our undertakings; and that it should be solitary; and above all that the especial season for it is the early morning'. Since this is a book about preaching, and not primarily about the spiritual life, we will not elaborate the theme further, but one or two books on the preacher's inner life are recommended in the bibliography.

The second picture Bunyan shows us is of someone with 'the best of books in his hand' and 'the Law of Truth written upon his lips'. The preacher is a man of the Book. Whenever I think of the preacher and his Bible I am reminded of the words of John Wesley:

> I want to know one thing, the way to heaven ... God himself has condescended to teach the way ... He hath written it down in a book. O give me that book: At any price give me the book of God! I have it: here is knowledge enough for me. Let me be *Homo unius libri* ... I sit down alone: only God is here. In his presence I open, I read his book; for to this end, to find the way to heaven ... Does any thing appear dark and intricate? I lift up my heart to the Father of Lights ... I then search after and consider parallel passages ... I meditate thereon ... If any doubt still remain, I consult those who are experienced in the things of God; and then the writings whereby, being dead, they yet speak. And what I thus learn, that I teach.

Not only is that a beautiful picture of the preacher's love for the Word of God, it is also a remarkably good account of the preaching process, and one we could well ponder. This centrality of the Bible in the life and work of the preacher need not surprise us, if we believe it to be the revelation of the heart and mind of God. James Stalker said, 'The more the Bible is searched, the more it will be loved; and the stronger will the conviction grow, that its deep truths are the Divine answers to the deep wants of human nature.' On this matter of the preacher's knowledge of and love for the Word of God, Stephen Neill has written:

> If you look back over the history of the Church, you will find that all the greatest preachers have been men whose

minds were steeped in the words of Scripture. Of Origen, the greatest scholar of the early Church, Bishop Westcott has remarked somewhere that he seems to have held the whole of Scripture in solution in his mind. Of St. John Chrysostom I read not long ago that in those great folio volumes of his sermons, which I cannot claim to have read *in extenso*, there are seven thousand quotations from the Old Testament, and eleven thousand from the New. Slight variations from the standard text of the Scriptures show that those great men generally quoted from memory; their minds were so full of Scripture that the words came naturally, and both thought and expression formed themselves according to the Scriptural pattern.

And Bishop Neill adds, 'I think you can always tell, listening to a preacher, whether he is a man of the Word or not, whether, that is to say, apart from quoting the Bible, he is really thinking biblically.'

I know of nothing which will inspire the preacher to be more diligent in his reading and studying of the Bible than the chapter 'On the study of the Bible' by John W. Burgon in *A Treatise on the Pastoral Office* (1864) (unless it be the same author's first sermon in his book *Inspiration and Interpretation* (1861)).

In Bunyan's picture the preacher also 'stood as if he pleaded with men'. Any preacher must have a great concern for humanity, and love for ordinary people.

We have before us the supreme example of our Master, who looked with compassion on the multitudes, because they were like sheep without a shepherd (Matthew 9:36), and who saw his own task in terms of being the Good Shepherd who lays down his life for the sheep.

We also have the example of Paul, whose love and concern for the Christians in the churches have always been an inspiration to pastors and teachers down the ages. And not the least remarkable quality in him is that despite his great intellectual powers, and his depths of soul, he had such a great love of the weak and often wayward people in the churches to which he wrote. It is not always so; sometimes those with great gifts of learning who are absorbed in great theological matters

are not able to enter into real relationships with ordinary
people. Yet Paul always made the recipients of his letters feel
that their concerns were his also, and he entered deeply into
their joys and sorrows.

'My dear children, for whom I am again in the pains of
childbirth until Christ is formed in you, how I wish I could be
with you now . . .' (Galatians 4:19).

'Therefore, my brothers, you whom I love and long for, my
joy and crown, that is how you should stand firm in the Lord,
dear friends!' (Philippians 4:1).

'For now we live, if ye stand fast in the Lord' (1 Thessalonians
3:8).

Dozens of other passages might be quoted to reveal Paul's
deep love for men. It is a most valuable exercise to read
through his letters to trace it out.

This quality of love for mankind is characteristic of so many
preachers that it is difficult to know where to make a choice.
Here is George Whitefield, arguably England's greatest preacher.

> The expressive eyes, the matchless voice, the trembling lips,
> the face that seemed to shine with a mystic light . . . were
> but the instruments and servants of a passionate and
> spiritual earnestness, such as seldom burned in a human
> soul . . . And through all Whitefield's oratory glowed –
> sometimes flamed – a passion of love for his hearers. 'You
> feel,' says Sir James Stephen, 'that you have to do with a
> man who lived and spoke, and who gladly would have died,
> to turn his hearers from the path of destruction and to guide
> them to holiness and peace.'
>
> W.H. Fitchett, *Wesley and his Century* (1906), p. 174

Once again, I find the gentle but firm advice by Bishop
Stephen Neill in his little book *On the Ministry* helpful at this
point. Although addressed to prospective ministers, it is
apposite to all who preach.

> If you are to be a successful minister of the Gospel, you
> must be able just to like folks. It is quite clear that our Lord
> liked folks. He enjoyed being with ordinary people. He did
> not go to the house of Mary and Martha and Lazarus in

order to fulfil a social duty; He went because He enjoyed being with His friends . . . He liked folks, and so must you. If you do not do it naturally, then you must learn to do it supernaturally. This care for people as individuals is essential to the work of the ministry [preaching] – so much so that I am sure that it is one of the gifts which we can ask of God in faith that it will be given. Some of us are naturally shy. That is a grievous handicap. But we must not lie down under it. It may not be possible for it to be completely cured. But I am sure that there is a great deal that God, in answer to prayer, is able to do about it.

Our last word in talking about the man behind the sermon must be to focus on the Holy Spirit. I am sure that no reader of this book will need to be reminded of the importance of the Holy Spirit to the preacher. From the very first page of the Bible where the Spirit of God broods over the waters, to the very last, where the Spirit of God inspires the Church's prayer for Christ to return, the Holy Spirit is active. To study the prophets is inevitably to see the importance of the Holy Spirit, since they spoke under his influence (see 2 Peter 1:21). Supremely, Jesus' ministry, his works of power, his words of teaching, his character, and his Passion and Resurrection, were all characterised by an inward grace and power which resulted from his being full of the Holy Spirit. He said as much at the very outset of his public ministry as he took to his lips the words of the Servant of the Lord, and quoted from Isaiah: 'The Spirit of the Lord is upon me, because he has anointed me to preach good news to the poor' (Luke 4:18, Isaiah 61:1). When we pass from the Gospels to the Acts of the Apostles, we are immediately aware of the presence of the Holy Spirit in a new and glorious way, as he empowers the Apostles in their preaching and evangelism. Not without reason has the book of Acts been called 'The Acts of the Holy Spirit'. But it is to Paul that we turn to see a plain statement connecting the Holy Spirit with the work of the preacher. Speaking about his own ministry, Paul says;

When I came to you, brothers, I did not come with eloquence or superior wisdom as I proclaimed to you the

testimony about God. For I resolved to know nothing while
I was with you except Jesus Christ and him crucified. I
came to you in weakness and fear, and with much trembling.
My message and my preaching were not with wise and
persuasive words, but with a demonstration of the Spirit's
power, so that your faith might not rest on man's wisdom,
but on God's power.

1 Corinthians 2:1-5

There is nothing in this passage which contradicts or
disparages learning, wisdom or eloquence. Paul himself had
all three in abundance. But in comparison with these qualities,
the power of the Holy Spirit is absolutely essential. For as he
says elsewhere in this chapter, only the Holy Spirit is able to
open a person's eyes to understand spiritual truths. It is not
something that the preacher can do merely by having good
material, a persuasive tongue and a winsome manner.

The preacher should be a person living by the Spirit (see, for
example, Galatians 5:16,25). As he prepares his messages, he
should look to the Spirit for his help, for the Spirit is the spirit
of knowledge, discernment and understanding (see Colossians
1:9), and it is the Spirit who inspired the Scriptures who must
give the illumination to understand them aright. This is seen
very beautifully in the passage where Jesus promises the
disciples the Holy Spirit.

When the Counsellor comes, whom I will send to you from
the Father, the Spirit of truth who goes out from the Father,
he will testify of me; but you also must testify. . .

John 15:26,27

The Spirit's work of bearing witness to the glory of the Son
is mirrored in the testimony of the disciples. It is their
testimony, combined with that of the Holy Spirit, which
brings glory to Jesus. Here we see that the testimony of the
Church (whether in its worship, its works of mercy, or in the
simple witness of ordinary believers, or in the preaching of the
Gospel) is an *essential* part of God's strategy. It is hardly
surprising that a preacher needs to pray for the Spirit's help in
the preparation of his messages.

But no less does the preacher need the Spirit to help him in the delivery of his message. We do not leave the Spirit behind in the study; he goes with us into the pulpit, and it is there that we need his touch of power to take our feeble words (for they are feeble, however carefully prepared) and wing them to the hearts of our listeners. Dr Martyn Lloyd-Jones spoke of Paul's phrase about 'the demonstration of the Spirit's power' like this:

> It is God giving power, and enabling, through the Spirit, to the preacher in order that he may do this work in a manner that lifts it up beyond the efforts and endeavours of man to a position in which the preacher is being used by the Spirit and becomes the channel through whom the Spirit works.

But our dependence upon the Spirit does not end with the conclusion of the sermon. For we know how easily in the hubbub that so often follows the end of the service, the seed of the Word of God can be snatched away by the enemy of souls. We need to pray that the Spirit will so lodge the seed in human hearts that it will spring up in renewed lives, acts of love and mercy, renewed determination to walk with God, or to reform lives, and convert men and women to new life in Christ. Most of us know that it is in this area that we most often neglect to pray. Having delivered our message, we are unlikely to follow it with prayer. Yet, we need to. Not in anxious worry about the success or failure of the sermon we have preached, but rather in committing the result to God the Holy Spirit who alone can bring life.

Much more might be said, for the character of the preacher is of such importance that it encompasses his holiness, his relationships with his hearers, his study of the Word of God and so on. The list of virtues necessary might be endlessly multiplied.

But one final thought will suffice. There is little doubt that given certain basic factors such as hard study, diligence, reflection and dependence upon the Holy Spirit, a preacher will improve his preaching. But he should at the same time strive to make progress in his Christian life, in the depth and quality of his spiritual life, and in his faith. 'Can two walk together, except they be agreed?' Amos' question rings in the preacher's ear. What a tragedy if the two things – the pulpit life and the devotional life – should grow apart.

Encore

As the pianist brings his recital to an end, the audience erupts in rapturous applause. He leaves the platform, but the applause continues, accompanied by shouts of 'Encore!' At first, it seems that the door to the platform will remain firmly closed, but after what seems several minutes (actually no more than one or two), the door opens and the pianist strides onto the stage, sits down at the piano and launches into a bravura encore. Although comparatively short, the impact on the audience is immense, and he is bombarded with demands for more. Depending on the pianist, he may respond with several. But eventually, he leaves the platform to return no more. The audience slowly disperses, dissatisfied that the performance will not continue for a further hour, but also deeply satisfied by the evening's bill of fare, knowing that the memory of this concert will remain a precious memory for years to come.

Not much like the average Sunday service, alas! Or so it would seem. A preacher may preach his heart out, and the only outward show of appreciation may be one or two words of thanks at the door. Yet wait a minute. When the preacher finished his sermon, his listeners didn't erupt in tumultuous applause. They didn't clamour for more. But if the preacher gave his soul, and had laboured over his sermon, and had prayed over it, what might have been the result? A defeated Christian made more aware of his resources in Christ, and given fresh determination to start again on the road of discipleship. A couple whose week had been bitter with angry words and accusations find their hands clasped, and reconciliation moving in their hearts. A young divorcee, who had come into church with a sense of loneliness and desolation and the future stretching out meaninglessly before her, discovers afresh that Jesus is her Bridegroom – the burden not entirely lifted, but significantly shifted from her shoulders to His. A man made aware of the waywardness of his life, and confronted with the living Christ, makes the great decision to commit his life to the Saviour. So often the results of preaching are unseen, silent and unheralded. Indeed, sometimes the positive results may not come to the preacher's notice until years afterwards – and sometimes never this side of eternity.

The joy of the preaching task is that we can give an encore. Next week we have another opportunity to open the Scriptures again. This week we felt dissatisfied with our effort: the structure was weak, and didn't reveal the inner truth of the text; the illustrations were weak, and the application somehow wasn't really on target. But the Lord 'who makes all things new' beckons us on, covers up our best efforts, and by his grace, makes our words the Bread of life.

For the preacher lives, like every Christian, by the promises of God. And there are so many promises about the Word of God and its effect that the preacher who ponders them cannot feel total discouragement for long.

> For you have been born again, not of perishable seed, but of imperishable through the living and enduring Word of God (Peter 1:23).

> As the rain and the snow come down from heaven.
> and do not return to it without watering the earth
> and making it bud and flourish,
> so that it yields seed for the sower and bread for the eater,
>   so is my word that goes out from my mouth;
> It will not return to me empty,
> but it will accomplish what I desire
> and achieve the purpose for which I send it (Isaiah 55:10–11).

> Listen! A farmer went out to sow his seed . . . Some fell on rocky places . . . But other seed fell on good soil. It came up, grew and produced a crop, multiplying thirty, sixty, or even a hundred times (Mark 4:3–8).

And with those encouraging words of Scripture, let me couple those of a wide and honoured preacher, Richard Cecil:

Christianity is so great and surprising in its nature that, in preaching it to others, I have no encouragement but in the belief of a continued divine operation. It is no difficult thing to change a man's opinions. It is no difficult thing to attach a man to my person and notions. It is no difficult thing to convert a proud man to spiritual pride, or a passionate man to passionate zeal for some religious party. But to bring a man to love God, to love the law of God while it condemns him, to loathe himself before God, to tread the earth under his feet, to hunger and thirst after God in Christ, and after the mind that was in Christ, this is impossible. But God has said it shall be done; and bids me go forth and preach, that by me, as His instrument, He may effect these great ends; and therefore I go.

Bibliography

Almost any book on preaching will provide some information and inspiration for the preacher. This bibliography is strictly limited. It is confined to books actually mentioned in the text, plus a few that may be regarded as indispensable for the beginning preacher. Those which might form a basic collection are marked with an asterisk.

BARNHOUSE, Donald Grey *Let Me Illustrate: Stories, Anecdotes, Illustrations* (Old Tappan, NJ, 1967).

*BAUMANN, J. D. *An Introduction to Contemporary Preaching* (Grand Rapids, 1972).

BREADY, J. W. *England Before and After Wesley* (London, 1938).

*BROOKS, P. *Eight Lectures on Preaching* (London, 1878; many editions).

BROWN, A. W. *Recollections of the Conversation Parties of the Rev. Charles Simeon* (London, 1863).

BROWNE, R. E. *The Ministry of the Word* (London, 1958).

BURGON, J. W. *A Treatise on the Pastoral Office* (London, 1864).

*COX, J. W. *Preaching* (San Francisco, 1985).

CRADDOCK, F. B. *Preaching* (Nashville, 1985).

*DAVIS, H. G. *Design for Preaching* (Philadelphia, 1958).

DUNCAN, G. B. *Wanting the Impossible* (London, 1957).

ELLIOT, E. *Twelve Baskets of Crumbs* (Nashville, 1976).

FITCHETT, W. H. *Wesley and his Century* (London, 1906).

JEFFS, E. H. *Princes of the Modern Pulpit* (London, 1931).

JOWETT, J. H. *The Preacher: His Life and Work* (London, 1912).

KER, J. *Thoughts for Heart and Life* Ed. A. L. Simpson (Edinburgh, 1888).

*KILLINGER, J. *Fundamentals of Preaching* (London, 1985).

*LLOYD-JONES, D. M. *Preaching and Preachers* (London, 1971).

LUCCOCK, H. E. *Christianity and the Individual in a World of Crowds* (Nashville, 1937); *Communicating the Gospel* (New York, 1954).

MACPHERSON, I. *The Art of Illustrating Sermons* (Nashville, 1964).

MORGAN, G. C. *Preaching* (London, 1937).

NEILL, S. C. *On the Ministry* (London, 1952).

PHILIP, A. *Lingering in the Sanctuary: Notes on John 14–17* (London 1936).

ROBINSON, H. W. *Biblical Preaching: the Development and Delivery of Expository Messages* (Grand Rapids, 1980).

SANGSTER, W. E. *The Craft of Sermon Construction* (London, 1949); *Power in Preaching* (London, 1958); *The Craft of Sermon Illustration* (London, 1946).

SCHERER, P. *The Word God Sent* (New York, 1965).

SMYTH, C. *The Art of Preaching: a Practical Survey of Preaching in the Church of England 1747–1939* (London, 1940).

*SPURGEON, C. H. *Lectures to my Students*, 3 vols. (London, 1875, 1877 & 1894; one-volume edition, Marshall Pickering, 1985).

STALKER, J. *The Preacher and his Models* (London, 1891).

STEWART, J. S. *Heralds of God* (London, 1946).

*STOTT, J.R.W. *I Believe in Preaching* (London, 1982). Also published in the USA under the title *Between Two Worlds; The Preacher's Portrait: Some New Testament Word Studies* (London, 1961).

*SWEAZEY, G. E. *Preaching the Good News* (Englewood Cliffs, NJ., 1976).

VINES, J. *A Guide to Effective Sermon Delivery* (Chicago, 1986).

Speech and allied topics

BURGESS, C. V. *Teach Yourself Speech Training* (London, 1960).

DUNKEL, J. and PARNHAM, E. *The Business Guide to Effective Speaking* (London, 1985).

HENDERSON, A. M. *Good Speaking* 2nd ed. (London, 1956).

SANGSTER, P. *Speech in the Pulpit* (London, 1958).

TURK, C. *Effective Speaking: Communicating in Speech* (London, 1985).

WESTLAND, P. *Teach Yourself Public Speaking* (London, 1946).

Some student preachers may wish to refresh their understanding of the English language and have some guidance on how to improve their writing skills. I recommend the following, which packs a lot into a small suitcase:

WALDHORN, A. & REIGER, A. *English Made Simple* (London, 1967).

The devotional life

The books that might be chosen under this heading are limitless. And in any case, books on the spiritual life are a very personal matter. Books that appeal to one person, leave another cold. Some people love the Puritans, others find them dry and dull. Some appreciate Catholic spirituality, and others find it anathema. I have chosen a small number of books, which I or my friends consider more or less indispensable. The reader will, of course, take his pick. I would also like to mention the value to the preacher of reading other men's sermons. No one can fail to profit *spiritually* from reading the sermons of such men as C. J. Vaughan, F. W. Robertson, C. H. Spurgeon, James Stewart, and Dr Martyn Lloyd-Jones (to name but a few). Certainly, in scouring second-hand bookshops, the inexperienced bookhunter is likely to pick up a lot of dross, as well as the occasional gold piece. But at least he will make his own discoveries.

I have given, where possible, the original date of publication. Most of these books, being classics, have been reprinted.

BAXTER, Richard *The Reformed Pastor* (1656). Possibly the greatest book ever written in English on the work of the pastor. For most modern-day readers an abridged edition (of which there have been many) is preferable.

BOUNDS, E. M. *Power through Prayer* (1920?).

BRIDGES, J. *The Pursuit of Holiness* (1978).

FOSTER, R. *Celebration of Discipline* (1980).

LLOYD-JONES, D. M. *Christian Warfare: Sermons on Ephesians 6:10–13* (1976); *The Christian Soldier: Sermons on Ephesians 6:10–20* (1977).

MACDONALD, G. *Restoring your Spiritual Passion* (1986).

MOULE, H.C.G. *To My Younger Brethren* (1892), esp. chaps. 1 and 2.

NOUWEN, H. *The Living Reminder* (1977).

PHELPS, A. *The Quiet Hour* (1860).

RYLE, J. C. *Holiness: its nature, hindrances, difficulties and roots* (1879; many reprints).

SCHAEFFER, F. *True Spirituality* (1972).

SPURGEON, C. H. *An All-round Ministry* (1960 reprint).